ENDORSEMENTS

I found this book to be a unique and much-needed look into how a married man should love his wife. Most marriage books hardly touch on this crucial aspect, especially from a male perspective. Too often, the topic is either glossed over or omitted altogether.

For the record, I consider Dr. Allen an expert on the subjects of marriage and relationships. Having led marriage workshops and seminars for years, he clearly knows what he's talking about.

— DR. JAMES R. LOVE, SR., COLLEGE & SEMINARY
PROFESSOR, MARRIED 45 YEARS

I will recommend this book to all of my clients—whether they are unmarried, avoiding marriage, or happily married. It's timeless, easy to read, and captures the true essence of what love really looks like.

— DR. IZOLA JONES, LICENSED CLINICAL
PROFESSIONAL COUNSELOR, MARRIED 55 YEARS

A great and easy read—I loved it! This book is a valuable resource to share with those who are struggling. It can be used in stages for young marriages and also serves as a powerful refresher for seasoned couples. In fact, many of the sections could be expanded into separate books because there's so much depth to explore!

— GAY GORDON, WIFE OF 40 YEARS

Dr. Jonathan Allen's *When a Man Really Loves a Woman* offers biblical wisdom, transparent insights, and practical coaching for husbands. This book equips men to love their wives with faith, honesty, and intentional action—an essential guide for any husband seeking to grow in godly love.

— Dr. Johnny Parker

If you're a man who wants to love better, this book gives you a clear, faith-rooted path forward. And if you're a woman reading along, it *will* make you reflect on what real, grounded love is supposed to feel like. That alone is powerful.

— Gail Keyes-Allen

It truly was a pleasure reading *When a Man Really Loves a Woman*. With every page, I thought, 'This is a man who gets it." It's so clear that he is a student of his wife. I'm definitely buying copies for the husbands I know. Well done!

— Natalie Blake, President & Chief Learning Officer, Inbibe Learning Company

WHEN A MAN REALLY LOVES A WOMAN

DR. JONATHAN W. ALLEN, SR.

FOREWORD BY
DR. WILLIE JOLLEY

ISBN: 979-8-9937355-0-4 (paperback)
ISBN: 979-8-9937355-1-1 (hardback)
LCCN: 2025903256

A NOTE TO THE READER

"IMPARTATIONS FOR MEN & RAISE EXPECTATIONS FOR WOMEN"

When a Man Really Loves a Woman was written first and foremost for men. It is a call to action, a roadmap, and a mirror—designed to help men rise into their God-ordained role as lovers, leaders, protectors, and partners. This book provides insight into the heart and mindset of a man who chooses covenant over comfort, commitment over convenience, and purpose over pride.

But while these pages speak directly to men, they are also meant to *raise the expectations* of the women reading them. If you're a woman holding this book, know that there is something here for you, too. You'll find language to articulate what your heart has longed for, clarity on what godly love looks like in action, and perhaps the courage to expect more —both from others and from yourself.

Whether you're single, married, divorced, or seeking to understand love through a biblical lens, you are welcome here.

Let's rediscover what it means to love and be loved—*God's way.*

*To my beautiful, anointed, and amazing wife for life,
Kimberely Yvette Reeder Allen...*

*You are my greatest blessing and the inspiration
behind every word of this book.*

"Love never fails..."

— 1 Corinthians 13:8

CONTENTS

FOREWORD

Love is one of the most powerful forces in the universe. It can heal, transform, and elevate every aspect of our lives. Yet, in a world filled with distractions and misunderstandings, love often requires intentionality, wisdom, and commitment to truly thrive.

Dr. Jonathan Allen's brilliant work, *When a Man Really Loves a Woman*, is not just a book—it's a heartfelt guide to understanding the depth and power of love when it's rooted in authenticity and purpose.

As someone who has spent decades inspiring others to overcome obstacles and build their best lives, I've learned that love is not just a feeling; it's an action, a decision, and an investment. In the marriage book I wrote with my wife Dee, entitled *Make Love, Make Money, Make It Last,* we say that love is a decision that starts with a foundation of being best friends that is grown through faith in God, and continues to build via great communication and mutual respect.

Dr. Allen dives deep into what it means to truly love— from the emotional vulnerability required to connect, to the sacrifices and joys of building a lasting partnership. In this book, he beautifully illustrates how a man's love, when grounded in integrity and sincerity, can not only uplift his partner, but also elevate his own life in the process. He challenges us men to step up, not just with words, but with actions that show honor, respect, and unwavering commitment.

What I admire most about this work is its honesty and practicality. It doesn't just talk about love in abstract terms; it gives tangible, relatable guidance for anyone seeking to love or be loved on a deeper level. Whether you're single, dating, married, or rebuilding a relationship, this book has wisdom for you.

Dr. Allen reminds us that love is more than romance—it's about building a foundation of trust, understanding, and shared purpose. He shows that when a man really loves a woman, he doesn't just seek to impress her; he seeks to protect, nurture, and grow alongside her.

This book is a must-read for any man who desires to love more effectively and for any woman who wants to understand what real love looks like from the man's perspective. It's a blueprint for those who are ready to move beyond surface-level relationships and embrace the transformative power of true love.

So, prepare your heart and mind for a journey of self-discovery, growth, and love. As you turn these pages, let the wisdom within them inspire you to create the kind of love that leaves a lasting legacy for generations to come.

Because... *when a man really loves a woman*, the world becomes a better place—not just for them, but for everyone around them and for generations yet unborn.

Dr. Willie Jolley
Hall of Fame Speaker
Sirius XM Radio Show Host

Bestselling Author of:
Rich Is Good, Wealthy Is Better
A Setback Is A Setup For A Comeback
An Attitude of Excellence
Make Love, Make Money, Make It Last!

PREFACE

Marriage is one of the most beautiful gifts God has given us. Yet, it's also one of the most challenging relationships we will ever experience. I know this firsthand. In the early years of my marriage, I thought love was enough. I believed that because I loved my wife, everything else would naturally fall into place. But love, while essential, isn't automatic. Love requires effort, intentionality, patience, and most importantly, a God-centered foundation.

I have been motivated by God to write this book to help and encourage as many people as possible so that their marriages will be so impacted by God that the trajectory will shift in a positive direction. That shift will move your relationship from challenging to good, from good to great, and from great to epic. This book is written to help and equip individuals who desire to be married, as well as couples in a pre-marital relationship or a marital covenant relationship, to fulfill God's plan for marriage.

 Therefore a man shall leave his father and mother and be joined to his wife, and they shall become one flesh.

— GENESIS 2:24

This book was born out of both personal experience and my years of counseling couples who have struggled to find joy and fulfillment in their marriages. I have sat across from countless husbands and wives, listening to their heartbreak, their frustration, and their longing to rediscover the love they once had. Through prayer, scripture, and practical steps, I've guided many couples back to a place of peace and intimacy—and now, I want to share those same principles with you.

Whether you are newly married, have been together for decades, preparing for marriage, or navigating a relationship, this book was designed to help you understand how a man should really love a woman. It's not about being perfect—it's about being *present*, *purposeful*, and *prayerful* in how that love is expressed, nurtured, and sustained.

Jonathan & Kimberely
40th Wedding Anniversary

INTRODUCTION

"YES, BUT THE FIRST TWO YEARS DON'T COUNT!"

When I think about our love story, my mind always goes back to when Kim and I first met when we were very young. We fell deeply in love and spent the next four years dating. Loving Kim was absolutely amazing. On our wedding day, I remember thinking: "Marrying the one you love must be like living in a fairytale. Life is going to be blissful forever."

But then life happened.

The first time I realized I had stepped into adulthood was the day I paid our first month's rent. Thirty days later, I was shocked when they expected the same amount again! That moment hit me hard—*this is real life.*

Though Kim and I loved each other tremendously, we didn't know how to love each other the way God intended. Life came at us fast, and I had to grow up quickly. I had to learn what it truly meant to take responsibility for providing for and caring for my wife.

The fairytale I had imagined was full of fun, laughter, and spontaneous vacations—basically, a lifelong honeymoon. But I hadn't considered the hard work required to build a marriage that truly thrives. The reality was very different. I worked multiple jobs just to keep up with bills.

It got so bad that, because of the constant arguments—especially over finances—and the harsh words we exchanged, Kim and I barely count those first few years when we tell people how long we've been happily married. Those early years were rough. But looking back, I'm thankful.

The painful lessons and hard truths I had to learn in those first two years became the foundation for everything I know about marriage today. And it burdens my heart to realize that so many men—at every stage of life—don't know how to really love a woman.

It wasn't until God laid it on our hearts to surrender all of our wrong expectations and preconceived ideas about marriage that things began to change. We had to let go of how we *thought* marriage should be and learn how to love each other in a way that honors God and brings joy to each other. This meant learning some hard, but necessary lessons about love and marriage.

The lessons I learned came from God's Word, observing other couples—both their successes and mistakes—and my own journey of growth. Over the years, these truths have shaped me as a husband, and now I want to share them with you so that you, too, can discover what it truly means *when a man really loves a woman.*

These are the ten lessons I learned:

Lesson #1: Marriage requires a covenant, not a contract.
Marriage isn't a transaction—it's a lifelong, unbreakable promise.

Lesson #2: Marriage requires a relationship, not roles. God designed marriage for connection and collaboration, not for rigid roles.

Lesson #3: Marriage requires hard work— and yes, it's worth it! Loving well takes effort, but it's worth every moment.

Lesson #4: Marriage requires you to really pay attention and effectively communicate. Listening is more than hearing —it's understanding with your heart. Listen first, then speak.

Lesson #5: Marriage requires emotional safety and trust. Trust is built through vulnerability, honesty, and consistency.

Lesson #6: Marriage requires protection and covering. Spiritually, emotionally, and physically— your wife should feel safe with you.

Lesson #7: Marriage requires prioritization. Love means putting your wife's well-being before your own desires.

Lesson #8: Marriage requires active support. Be your wife's biggest cheerleader and celebrate her wins.

Lesson #9: Marriage requires spiritual strength. Keep God at the center of your relationship.

Lesson #10: Marriage requires daily forgiveness and grace. Love thrives where grace and forgiveness abound.

These ten lessons are specifically directed towards men and serve as the foundation for everything I share in this book, guiding you through the key principles for building a lasting and fulfilling marriage. The struggles, the failures, and the victories in my marriage aren't just stories— they're practical tools and timeless truths designed to guide men toward becoming the kind of husband God calls them to be and to help women recognize the love they truly deserve.

While each of these lessons is explored individually, they are deeply interconnected. Loving well is not a series of isolated actions, but a reflection of a heart aligned with God's design. Communication strengthens trust. Prioritizing your wife's needs deepens emotional safety. Spiritual leadership influences how you protect, serve, and support your wife.

This book is not a checklist but a guide to lifelong growth. As you apply these lessons, you'll see how one area of love naturally strengthens another. Progress in one area leads to progress in others. Some lessons will challenge you more than others, and that's okay. Growth is a process, not a destination.

For the men reading this, my prayer is that you will embrace these lessons and truly learn how to love a woman the way God designed—sacrificially, unconditionally, and faithfully. Whether you're married or preparing for marriage, I challenge you to examine your heart.

> If you're *married*, are you showing up fully for your wife—not just in words but in consistent actions? Are you loving her as Christ loves the Church, with sacrificial and unwavering commitment? Are you building a foundation of trust, respect, and spiritual strength that can withstand any challenge?

> If you're *single*, is your heart being prepared to love a woman with this kind of intentionality? Are you becoming the man God is calling you to be—one who leads with humility, loves with patience, and serves with strength?

For the women reading this, my prayer is that you will raise your expectations and never settle for less than God's best. You deserve a love that reflects God's design—a man who will lead with grace, love with sacrifice, and honor you in every season.

This book is not only to encourage men to love well, but also to empower women to never settle for less than God's intention. Let this be your invitation to pursue, experience, and expect a love that honors God and transforms lives.

* * *

Let's begin this journey of learning how
a man *really* loves a woman.

PART ONE

A GODLY FOUNDATION

A strong, thriving marriage isn't accidental—it's built on a God-centered foundation. Before a man can really love a woman as God designed, he must understand that marriage is a sacred covenant, not a conditional contract. It's about prioritizing genuine relationship over societal roles and loving with commitment, respect, and friendship. Marriage takes effort and sacrifice, but when rooted in God's truth, it becomes a bond that weathers any storm and brings lasting joy.

In this section, we'll explore how to lay this godly foundation by:

- *Living in covenant, not in contract*—committing fully and unconditionally to your spouse, as God intended
- *Building on relationship, not roles*—focusing on friendship and partnership, rather than rigid expectations
- *Embracing the hard work of marriage (and why it's worth it)* — understanding that lasting love takes effort but leads to lifelong fulfillment

LESSON # 1

HOW TO LIVE IN COVENANT, NOT IN CONTRACT

Marriage is one of God's most profound gifts, a covenant that mirrors His unchanging love.

— PASTOR DUKE TABER

Marriage is not a 50/50 relationship. Marriage is not about keeping score or meeting each other halfway. That kind of thinking reduces marriage to a contract—a transactional agreement where both parties contribute only if the other does. But God designed marriage to be a covenant, not a contract.

A contract is built on mutual benefit and is easily broken when one side doesn't hold up their end. A covenant, however, is a sacred, lifelong commitment to God. Both partners must faithfully uphold this covenant in order for the marriage to continually flourish and deepen in God. God's design for marriage calls for 100% commitment from both partners—not conditional love that is performance-based.

 Therefore a man shall leave his father and mother and be joined to his wife, and they shall become one flesh.

— GENESIS 2:24

When we look at marriage through God's eyes, it becomes clear that love is more than just an emotion—it's a daily choice. The Word of God instructs husbands:

 Husbands, love your wives, just as Christ also loved the church and gave Himself for her.

— Ephesians 5:25

This type of love is sacrificial and unconditional. A healthy, loving relationship between a husband and wife is never transactional. I don't love my wife with the expectation of receiving something in return, and I certainly don't withhold my love when she doesn't meet my expectations. True love is about giving freely and selflessly. My commitment is to consistently bring my best to our marriage—showing up every day with intentional love and unwavering support, regardless of our circumstances.

This is what it means to love unconditionally—to give without keeping score or expecting anything in return.

Shift From Contract to Covenant

When a man really loves a woman, he shifts from a contractual mindset to a covenant mindset. When he does that, everything changes.

- *Conflicts* are resolved with grace instead of resentment.
- *Sacrifices* are made willingly, not begrudgingly.
- *Love* deepens because it's rooted in God's design, not worldly expectations.

Marriage isn't about fairness— it's about faithfulness. If you want a marriage that thrives, start by embracing the covenant God created. Let go of the idea that marriage is a transactional exchange. Instead, step into your calling to love your wife with the same selfless, sacrificial love that Christ has for the Church.

TAKE RESPONSIBILITY AS A COVENANT LEADER

When a man really loves a woman, he takes responsibility for his words and actions, instead of blaming her or others. Being the head of the relationship means owning both successes and failures. It means refusing to pass the blame. A man cannot fall into the *"Adam complex"* like in Genesis when Adam deflected responsibility onto Eve.

 Then the man said, 'The woman whom You gave to be with me, she gave me of the tree, and I ate.'

— GENESIS 3:12

A loving husband leads with integrity. He accepts full responsibility for his role in the marriage. He doesn't shift blame—he steps up. Leadership in marriage isn't about control; it's about accountability. A man who loves his wife deeply understands that his role is to protect, nurture, and lead with humility and strength.

* * *

In the next chapter, we'll explore the difference between *roles* and *relationships* in marriage—and how embracing both can strengthen your bond and bring you closer together.

How to Build On Relationship, Not Roles

Marriage is a journey, and it becomes beautiful when traveled hand in hand with Christ at the center.

— UNKNOWN

In marriage, it's easy to fall into the trap of rigidly defined roles. Society often dictates that husbands should act a certain way, while wives are expected to fulfill specific duties. However, God's design for marriage goes beyond roles—it is built on relationship.

When marriage is driven solely by traditional roles, it can unintentionally create distance rather than intimacy. A husband may believe that providing financially is enough, while a wife may feel her responsibility is limited to managing the home. But God calls husbands and wives to be partners, friends, and companions in every aspect of life.

 Two are better than one, because they have a good reward for their labor. For if they fall, one will lift up his companion...

— ECCLESIASTES 4:9

A thriving marriage is built on partnership. This doesn't mean that roles are irrelevant—but rather that they should never overshadow the friendship, emotional intimacy, and mutual support that sustain a strong relationship.

BALANCE YOUR ROLE & RELATIONSHIP

When a man really loves a woman, he will be balanced in every area of his life. God designed husbands to lead with love and humility; he designed wives to support with strength and grace. Yet, this dynamic isn't about dominance or blind submission—it's about partnership. A husband's leadership should reflect Christ's servant-hearted leadership, and a wife's support should reflect the strength and dignity God instills in her.

Balance is key. Responsibilities must be shared and adjusted without sacrificing the emotional and spiritual connection that keeps the marriage alive. When both spouses invest in their relationship, they grow together in every way—spiritually, emotionally, and physically.

BUILD A FRIENDSHIP IN MARRIAGE

When a man really loves a woman, he will be her best friend. At its core, marriage should be a deep friendship where both individuals genuinely enjoy each other's company. Building and maintaining that friendship involves:

- *Spending Quality Time Together:* Whether it's a date night, shared hobbies, or even simple conversations, intentional time fosters connection.

- *Supporting Each Other's Goals:* Encouraging each other's dreams and ambitions builds mutual respect and admiration.

- *Communicating Openly:* Honest conversations about thoughts, feelings, and struggles deepen emotional intimacy.

A strong friendship creates a safe and loving space where both partners feel valued and understood.

DON'T BUILD BARRIERS

When a man really loves a woman, he will not allow his role to become a barrier. Sometimes, couples become so focused on fulfilling traditional roles that they neglect the relationship itself. This can lead to feelings of isolation, frustration, and even resentment. To prevent this, couples must:

- *Reevaluate Responsibilities:* Adjust and adapt roles as seasons of life change.

- *Share the Load:* Work together in managing the home, raising children, and navigating life's demands.

- *Ensure Mutual Value:* Make sure neither partner feels overlooked, underappreciated, or undervalued.

Marriage is not about rigid roles—it's about shared responsibility, mutual respect, and growing together in love.

EMBRACE GOD'S DESIGN FOR RELATIONSHIP

When a man really loves a woman, he will honor God through his love for his woman. Marriage is designed to reflect God's relationship with us— overflowing with grace, love, and companionship. In Ephesians 5:21, Paul writes, *"Submit to one another out of reverence for Christ."* This mutual submission creates unity and eliminates the power struggles that can arise when roles are misunderstood or misused.

When both spouses serve each other with love and humility, they cultivate a marriage that honors God and brings lasting joy.

SEEK UNDERSTANDING, NOT CHANGE

When a man really loves a woman, he will avoid trying to change her personality. Instead, he seeks to understand and appreciate who she is.

God created each of us with unique traits and qualities. While destructive behaviors should be addressed, a person's core personality should be loved and accepted. A loving relationship fosters an environment where both people can grow and thrive.

Trying to change someone often leads to frustration and distance. Instead, when a man truly loves a woman, he actively works to understand her deeply and supports her growth. This requires patience, curiosity, and intentional connection.

 Therefore receive one another, just as Christ also received us, to the glory of God.

— ROMANS 15:7

The most effective way to grow in understanding is through meaningful conversation, prayer, and intentional listening. Counseling and therapy can also be valuable tools to support growth and communication in marriage. This will deepen your understanding of your wife, so that you can love her the way God intended.

REFLECT AND ACT

When a man really loves a woman, he will schedule regular time to think. Intentional time spent thinking can be instrumental in the overall growth of your marriage.

Ask yourself:

- Am I prioritizing our relationship over rigid expectations?
- Do I truly understand and appreciate my wife's personality, strengths, and struggles?
- How can I better support and encourage my wife's growth?

Marriage thrives when both partners are committed to nurturing their friendship, balancing responsibilities, and building emotional intimacy.

* * *

In the next chapter, we will explore why *marriage is hard work*—and why that's not a bad thing. Embracing the effort it takes to build a strong, lasting marriage is key to deepening your connection and growing together in Christ.

HOW TO EMBRACE THE HARD WORK OF MARRIAGE (YES, IT'S WORTH IT!)

Marriage was originally intended to be a covenant between a man, a woman, and God —for a lifetime.

— PASTOR PAUL BROWN

Let's face it: marriage is hard work—and that's perfectly okay! Building a marriage that honors God and brings lasting joy requires intentional, consistent effort. It's easy to fall into the trap of expecting marriage to be effortless, especially when we imagine a life full of love, laughter, and romance. But the truth is, a thriving marriage is not built on feelings alone; it's built on daily choices, sacrifice, and perseverance.

Selfishness has no place in marriage. God didn't bring you and your spouse together to fix or change each other. He joined you together to complement, complete, and strengthen one another. A strong marriage is formed when both partners are willing to work for the love they desire.

Love What She Loves

When a man really loves a woman, he will learn to love what she loves. As a husband, one key to making marriage work is learning to love what your wife loves. For example, I love riding motorcycles. While my wife Kim may not share my passion, she rides with me because she loves me. Likewise, Kim enjoys going to the movies. Although it's not my favorite activity, I cherish those moments with her because it brings her joy.

It's not about always loving the same things—it's about valuing what matters to each other and finding ways to show love through shared experiences. Small sacrifices like these strengthen the bond between husband and wife.

Fight For — Not Against Her

When a man really loves a woman, he will fight for her. One of the greatest lessons I've learned is that when challenges arise, a man must fight *for* his wife—*not against* her.

Marriage comes with disagreements, but your spouse is never the enemy. The real enemy seeks to divide and destroy marriages by sowing seeds of offense, misunderstanding, and resentment. In moments of conflict, remind yourself and your wife that you are on the same team.

Pause, pray, and protect your wife. Cover your wife in prayer and shield her from emotional harm. As her husband, God calls you to be her protector and defender, not her adversary.

Remember That She's Your Teammate

When a man really loves a woman, he will see her as his partner. It is vitally important to remember that the person you love is on the same team as you. In marriage, you and your spouse share:

- *The same Owner* — God
- *The same coach* — Pastor
- *The same uniforms* — represents unity in the relationship
- *The same side of the field* — working together in partnership

- *The same corner* — support through every challenge

Your pastor is often one of your biggest supporters in your marriage. A trustworthy pastor takes the responsibility of confidentiality seriously, offering guidance and support when challenges arise. Don't hesitate to seek counsel or be directed to someone who can help strengthen your marriage.

Men, it's crucial to repeat that the woman you love knows you are *always fighting with her and for her*—never against her. She is your partner, not your opponent. What an incredible privilege it is to have someone by your side to fight life's battles together.

Let me make this clear: *Your spouse is not your enemy.* An enemy is someone who is antagonistic or hostile. That's not who your wife is. The woman you love is attached to you by deep affection and esteem. When conflict arises, focus on solving the problem, not attacking the person.

The Word of God reminds us:

> For we do not wrestle against flesh and blood, but against principalities, against powers, against the rulers of the darkness of this age, against spiritual hosts of wickedness in the heavenly places.
>
> — EPHESIANS 6:12

Sometimes, the problem isn't your spouse—it's your own attitude or behavior. Take a moment to look in the mirror and reflect. Here's a simple reminder to speak over your relationship during conflict:

- *I am not the enemy.*
- *You are not the enemy.*
- *Together, we will defeat the enemy of our souls.*

Break Down Walls of Division

When a man really loves a woman, he will alleviate any walls of division. Unresolved conflicts can build invisible walls in marriage—walls that separate rather than unite. Some of these walls include:

- *Unfulfilled Expectations, Unimplemented Plans, and Unkept Promises:* Small disappointments can lead to major disagreements if left unaddressed.

- *Unmet Needs, Unprized Gifts, and Unrecognized Sacrifices:* Failing to meet your wife's emotional needs or appreciate her sacrifices can make her feel unseen and unloved.

- *Unhealed Hurts, Unresolved Anger, and Unrepented Offenses:* When hurtful words or actions go unaddressed, resentment can take root.

- *Unconfessed Sin, Undignified Communication, and Unfeeling Responses:* Hidden sins and careless words damage trust and intimacy.

These walls create a cycle of mistrust, leading to emotional distance and conflict. Your wife needs to know that you are her greatest ally, standing beside her in every battle.

Turn Conflict into Connection

When a man really loves a woman, he will seek win-win resolutions to personal conflicts. Conflict is inevitable in any relationship, but how you handle it can either strengthen or weaken your marriage. A man who truly loves a woman doesn't fight to win an argument—he seeks solutions that strengthen the relationship. His goal isn't to be right, but to be united.

In the article *"Are Your Relationships Too Competitive? Try Shifting to Win/Win"* by Khang Tran, the author emphasizes the power of win-

win thinking in relationships, drawing from Stephen Covey's *7 Habits of Highly Effective People.* These habits offer powerful strategies for resolving conflict in ways that deepen love and trust.

Here's how you can apply these habits to your marriage:

√ Habit # 1: Be Proactive

Take responsibility for your actions and interactions. You are fully responsible for your words, actions, and reactions. No one—*not even your wife*—controls how you feel or behave. A man who really loves a woman takes ownership of his role in conflict and doesn't blame her for his emotional state.

It's time to "put your big boy pants on" and step up. Own your responsibility in your marriage—to your wife, your family, your church, and your community. Real love requires maturity and accountability.

√ Habit 2: Begin with the End in Mind

Focus on building a stronger relationship, not winning the fight. Ask yourself, "What outcome do I want from this conflict?" If your goal is a stronger, healthier marriage, then your actions must reflect that. It's not about proving your point but working together for a solution that honors both of you.

When your focus shifts from "winning" to "loving," conflicts turn into opportunities for growth. Love always seeks the best for the other person.

✓ Habit 3: Put First Things First

Prioritize your relationship over being right. Before you react, ask yourself the following questions:

- Will this argument bring us closer or push us apart?
- Will she feel loved and valued after this conversation?
- Will I regret my words or actions later?

Address issues with love and humility. If unresolved pain or misunderstanding lingers, don't be afraid to seek counseling. Prioritize the health of your marriage above pride or ego.

✓ Habit 4: Think Win-Win

True collaboration happens when two people build a foundation of deep trust and genuinely seek the best outcome for each other. When a man truly loves a woman, he is committed to her success and happiness, striving for solutions that benefit them both. In turn, she is inspired to work just as hard to support and uplift him, creating a relationship where both partners thrive together.

✓ Habit 5: Seek to Understand First, Then Understood

Listen with love before speaking. Listening is a game-changer in conflict resolution. Don't listen to respond—listen to understand. Love is shown when you truly hear your wife's heart, not just her words.

Practice the 80/20 rule in communication: listen 80% of the time and speak only 20%. Replace lecturing with affirming words. Show her that what she feels matters deeply to you.

✓ Habit 6: Synergize

Work together to strengthen your bond. Conflict doesn't have to drive you apart—it can bring you closer when you face it together. Engage in activities that foster teamwork and open communication.

Enjoy shared hobbies: cooking, gardening, DIY projects, or even watching a favorite show. Building something together— whether it's a home project or emotional intimacy—deepens connection.

Marriage is a partnership. Approach conflict as teammates, not opponents.

✓ Habit 7: Sharpen the Saw

Prioritize self-care so you can fully show up in your marriage. You can't pour into your wife if you're running on empty. Taking care of your physical, emotional, and spiritual health allows you to be the best version of yourself for her.

Exercise, spend time in prayer, and invest in personal growth. A healthy man creates a healthy marriage. Remember, *love wins when you both win!*

When a man really loves a woman, he doesn't fight to win arguments—he fights for connection. Conflict handled with love can strengthen trust, deepen intimacy, and create lasting unity. Love isn't about keeping score; it's about creating solutions where both hearts win.

Choose to fight *for* your marriage, *not in* it.

Marriage is hard work, but it is the most rewarding work you will ever do. The time, effort, and love you invest in your marriage will bear fruit for a lifetime.

Be Patient and Flexible

When a man really loves a woman, he becomes a patient partner with a persistent pursuit. Patience and flexibility are the glue of marriage. Marriage requires more than love—it demands patience and flexibility. Women, like men, go through emotional shifts, changing thoughts, and evolving goals. A man who truly loves a woman must be adaptable, persevering, and flexible. He must continue to provide and pursue her with intentionality, even when seasons change.

Flexibility

Flexibility is a powerful trait that strengthens a relationship. It fosters an environment where both partners feel respected, understood, and deeply connected. When the woman you love shifts, you must be willing to shift with her—embracing her changes with love and grace.

Let me share a personal story:

Throughout much of our marriage, my wife, Kim, wasn't fond of the outdoors or animals. But when she turned 50, something changed—she wanted a dog. One day, I came home and saw her lying in the grass, happily playing with our new dog, Pinkkim. I remember thinking, *Who is this woman I'm married to today?*

In that moment, I had a choice: resist the change or embrace it. I chose to lean in. I became a proud and loving "Dog Dad" to Pinkkim because loving Kim meant adapting to what brought her joy. This shift required patience and persistence, but it deepened our bond.

Flexibility in marriage means being:

- *Open to Change:* Embracing the evolving needs and desires of your spouse.
- *Willing to Take Risks:* Stepping outside your comfort zone to support your partner.
- *Ready to Adapt and Adjust:* Changing behaviors and mindsets without compromising core values.

Patience

Patience isn't optional—it's essential. A loving husband must practice patience to truly nurture his marriage. Patience keeps the relationship meaningful, engaging, and full of grace. I often say that patience is God's glue—it holds marriages together for the long haul.

After more than forty years of marriage, I can say with certainty that Kim had to be patient with me, just as I had to be patient with her. Relationships are a constant work in progress. W.H. Auden once said, *"Perhaps there is only one cardinal sin: impatience. Because of impatience, we were driven out of Paradise; because of impatience, we cannot return."*

The Bible reminds us:

 Love suffers long and is kind; love does not envy; love does not parade itself, is not puffed up.

— 1 CORINTHIANS 13:4

Patience in marriage means trusting God to continue His work in your spouse. Like clay on the potter's wheel, your partner is constantly being shaped by God. Your role is to stand by them patiently, knowing the masterpiece is still in progress.

Here's the truth: God isn't finished with you or your spouse. And because of that, patience isn't a one-time decision—it's a lifelong commitment.

So, when a man really loves a woman, he patiently waits, persistently pursues, and gracefully adapts. And through it all, love only grows stronger.

Put in the Work

When a man really loves a woman, he will understand that his marriage is worth the effort. Marriage is hard work, but it is holy work. The time, effort, and love you invest in your marriage will yield fruit for a lifetime.

The reality is this:

- Marriage requires intentional effort.
- Marriage requires sacrifice.
- Marriage requires grace.

Every moment spent building, forgiving, and loving is worth it.

* * *

In the next part of this book, we will explore how to deepen *emotional connection* and build *spiritual intimacy* with your spouse. Loving your wife is not just about hard work—it's about heart work. And it's the most rewarding work you will ever do.

Let's keep building.

Part Two

Communication & Connection

A marriage without meaningful communication is like a house without a foundation—unstable and vulnerable to collapse. Words have the power to build or break, heal or hurt, draw closer or push away. Communication is more than just talking. It's about listening, paying attention, and being intentional with your words and actions. Connection happens when both partners feel seen, heard, and understood. It's built in the small moments—when you listen without interrupting, notice the little things, and make your spouse feel emotionally safe.

In this section, we'll share how to:

- *Listen with purpose* to understand your spouse's needs
- *Communicate with love and clarity* to avoid misunderstandings
- *Create emotional safety* where trust and vulnerability can grow
- *Pay attention* to the little things that deepen intimacy and respond with love
- *Resolve conflict* with grace and *rebuild trust* through forgiveness

LESSON # 4

HOW TO REALLY PAY ATTENTION AND RESPOND

L ove is often found in the smallest gestures. In marriage, it's not the grand gestures that sustain a relationship, but the everyday moments of thoughtfulness and care. When a man truly loves a woman, he pays close attention. It's the way he remembers her favorite meal after a long day or surprises her with small comforts that speak louder than words. These intentional acts, though seemingly small, build a foundation of trust, affection, and lasting connection. Love thrives in the details, and a man who notices and responds to those details nurtures a marriage that grows stronger with time.

PAY ATTENTION TO SMALL DETAILS

When a man truly loves a woman, he pays attention to the details that make her feel loved, seen, and valued. It's often the little things that make the biggest difference in marriage. Small, intentional acts of love speak louder than grand gestures because they show thoughtfulness, attentiveness, and consistent care.

It's easy to overlook the small things in the busyness of life, but those little moments and thoughtful actions build a foundation of trust and affection. Noticing and acting on the small details of your wife's likes and dislikes can deeply strengthen your bond.

For me, this attentiveness shows up in two specific ways:

1. Knowing Her Favorite Restaurants

I keep a list of all the restaurants Kim loves in the notes on my phone. When she enjoys a place, I add it to the list. If she doesn't like it, I make a note: "Do not return." This simple habit allows me to plan dates and surprise her with meals I know she'll love. It's not about the restaurant—it's about showing her that her preferences matter to me.

2. Remembering Her Favorite Perfumes

Kim loves perfume, and because of that, I've made it a point to remember every fragrance she enjoys. I keep a running list of her favorites so when it's time for a gift or a special occasion, I know exactly what to get. It's a simple gesture, but it tells her, "I notice you. I care about what makes you feel good."

Loving your wife well means studying her—learning what brings her joy, what causes her stress, and what comforts her in difficult moments. Treat this as if you're preparing for the most important exam of your life.

Ask yourself:

- *Does she sigh and shake her head when she walks into a messy kitchen?* Maybe it's time to step in and help tidy up before she says a word.

- *Does she light up when you offer a neck rub after a long day?* Small physical gestures can communicate love and care in ways words cannot.

- *Does she need quiet time after work, or does she prefer to talk about her day right away?* Paying attention to these routines and preferences makes her feel understood.

Here are some practical ways to show your wife you're tuned in to her needs and desires:

1. Notice her mood changes.

Pay attention to her energy and emotions. Is she more quiet than usual? Is she extra chatty? These shifts might be clues that she needs your support or space.

2. Learn her comforts.

Know what relaxes her—a favorite drink, a cozy blanket, or a specific show she loves. Surprise her with these comforts when she's had a tough day.

3. Anticipate her needs.

If she's mentioned needing new shoes or wanting to reorganize a room, take the initiative to help. Anticipation shows attentiveness.

4. Celebrate her small wins.

Whether it's completing a project at work or managing a tough day with the kids, acknowledge and celebrate her efforts.

It's not the expensive gifts or lavish vacations that sustain a marriage — it's the everyday moments of care and attention. When a man really loves a woman, he chooses to love her in small, meaningful ways, every single day.

By noticing and responding to these small cues, you're saying, "I see you. I hear you. I value you." This kind of love fosters deep trust, emotional safety, and lasting connection.

PAY ATTENTION TO NON-VERBAL COMMUNICATION

When a man really loves a woman, he notices her body language, posture, and expression— and responds appropriately. Words are powerful, but so much of communication happens without them. In fact, experts estimate that 80-90% of all communication is non-verbal. This means that what your wife says with her body language, facial expressions, tone of voice, and even how she dresses often speaks louder than her words.

When a man truly loves a woman, he becomes a student of her non-verbal cues. He pays attention to the small shifts in her expressions, the tone behind her words, and the silent signals she sends. Recognizing these unspoken messages allows a husband to respond with love, understanding, and intentional care.

When a man really loves a woman, he will:

1. *Notice her facial expressions:* Pay attention to the subtle shifts in her expressions. Does a raised eyebrow signal concern or curiosity? Does a sigh indicate exhaustion or frustration? These small cues reveal how she's truly feeling.

2. *Watch her body language*: Is she crossing her arms in frustration or leaning away during a conversation? Body language often communicates discomfort or disconnection. Respond with warmth and openness rather than defensiveness.

3. *Listen to her tone of voice:* Sometimes it's not what she says, but how she says it. A soft tone may mean she needs comfort, while a sharp tone might indicate she feels unheard.

4. *Understand Her Trigger Words:* Certain phrases or words can carry emotional weight. Learn what topics or statements trigger

strong reactions and approach those conversations with sensitivity.

5. Recognize the messages in her appearance: How your wife presents herself can reflect her mood. If she's usually put together but seems disheveled, she might be overwhelmed. If she's dressed up more than usual, she might be seeking your attention or affirmation.

6. Recognize her silence: Sometimes, "Nothing is wrong" isn't the full story. Silence can speak volumes, and it's important to approach it with patience and care.

After more than 40 years of marriage, I can tell when Kim's mood shifts. I know when her vocal tone softens, when her facial expression changes, or when her body language feels distant. In those moments, I step into what I call "investigation mode"—not to pry but to understand. I ask myself:

- Do I need to *pray* for her about something weighing on her heart?
- Do I need to *apologize* for something I may have said or done?
- Do I need to simply be *patient* and give her space until she's ready to share?

This kind of attentiveness doesn't happen overnight. It requires daily effort and intentionality.

The Word of God reminds us:

> So then, my beloved brethren, let every man be swift to hear, slow to speak, slow to wrath; for the wrath of man does not produce the righteousness of God.

> — JAMES 1:19-20

This Scripture offers a blueprint for how we should approach communication—especially with our wives. Listening is not just about hearing words; it's about observing, understanding, and responding thoughtfully.

When we slow down and truly listen—both to what's said and what's unsaid—we create a safe space for our wives to be vulnerable and honest. This kind of attentive listening builds trust, fosters emotional security, and deepens intimacy. It goes far beyond words; it requires being a student of her heart.

Loving a woman means being attentive to her heart in every way. Learn her looks, her moods, and her non-verbal signals— then respond with patience and compassion. Over time, this attentiveness will strengthen your connection and show her that she is truly loved and understood.

LEARN TO REALLY LISTEN

When a man really loves a woman, he listens to understand—not just to respond. One of the greatest acts of love is the gift of truly listening. Too often, we engage in conversations with the intention of defending our point or preparing our next argument. This mindset blocks us from fully understanding what our wife is expressing. Real communication requires more than just hearing words—it demands our full presence, focus, and intentionality.

When your wife speaks, don't mentally prepare a rebuttal or think about how you'll respond before she's finished. Instead, give her your full attention. Lean in. Listen not only to her words but also to the emotions behind them.

If we're honest, many of us have been guilty of tuning out, nodding along while our minds are elsewhere. I've done it, too. As a multi-tasker, I often juggle several things at once. Kim has caught me more than once and lovingly said, "Hey, you're not focused on what I'm talking about. You're thinking about something else."

Moments like that remind me how important it is to give her my full attention. Intentional listening tells her she is valued, loved, and worth my undivided focus.

Communication isn't just about words. Much of what your wife feels is communicated through her non-verbal cues. Her facial expressions, tone of voice, and even her body language reveal what's truly on her heart.

Kim's expressions often tell me more than her words. A raised eyebrow, a sigh, or a subtle frown can speak volumes. It's in these small details that we learn how to respond with love and care.

Here are some intentional steps to help you become a better listener:

- *Be present:* Eliminate distractions. Put down your phone, turn off the TV, and give her your full attention. Make eye contact and lean in—show her that she has your undivided focus.

- *Reflect on what you hear:* Clarify what she's saying by repeating it back in your own words. Use phrases like, "What I hear you saying is…" or "It sounds like you're feeling…" This not only shows you're listening but also ensures you're understanding her correctly.

- *Observe non-verbal cues:* Pay attention to her tone, expressions, and body language. Often, her emotions are more visible in what she doesn't say.

- *Resist the urge to fix:* Sometimes your wife doesn't need you to solve the problem—she needs you to listen. Validate her feelings instead of immediately offering solutions. You can ask, "Do you want me to listen or help you find a solution?"

- *Pause before responding:* Take a moment to think before you speak. A thoughtful response shows respect and care, while a rushed reply can feel dismissive.

- *Ask thoughtful questions:* Show genuine interest by asking open-ended questions. For example, "How did that make you feel?" or "What do you think we should do next?"

Listening is more than a communication tool—it's a way to love your wife deeply. It's a way of saying, "You matter to me. Your thoughts, your feelings, and your words are important."

Don't Judge— Respond with Love

When a man loves a woman, he listens without judgment and always responds with the truth in love. Mother Teresa once said: "If you judge people, you have no time to love them."

Being judgmental is a powerful, destructive force in any relationship. When a man truly loves a woman, he must avoid being judgmental if he desires a healthy, thriving connection. Judgment occurs when we refuse to accept another person's words or actions and instead impose our own thoughts, opinions, and mindsets onto them. This creates distance and breeds resentment. In contrast, genuine love involves responding in truth with compassion—offering guidance, support, and encouragement in a way that uplifts rather than criticizes. A loving man understands that his role is not to judge, but to nurture, helping the woman he loves grow and thrive in a safe and supportive environment.

As your beloved's cheerleader, continually find endless ways to encourage, edify, and build up your beloved. You want to live this out in word and deed with your beloved.

Every truth and encouragement that could
have made a difference to you, you got it from me.

The Word of God teaches us:

 But, speaking the truth in love, may grow up in all things into Him who is the head—Christ.

— Ephesians 4:15

Maturity in marriage means learning to communicate truth with love and grace. Speaking the truth in love fosters open and honest communication, where both spouses feel safe to express their needs, thoughts, and concerns.

DON'T BE DEFENSIVE— RESPOND WITH PATIENCE

When a man really loves a woman, he refuses to allow his communication to become defensive. A man who truly loves a woman understands that defensiveness can be destructive to healthy communication. Instead of reacting impulsively or defensively, he chooses to respond with patience, humility, and understanding.

In his article, "How to Stop Being Defensive: A Simple 6-Step Process," Jack Nollan offers practical strategies for managing defensiveness in relationships. Here are some of his key insights, along with biblical principles to guide your communication:

1. Pause and Breathe Before Responding

Scripture reminds us to be "quick to listen, slow to speak, and slow to become angry" (James 1:19, NIV). Speaking too quickly —especially in anger or anxiety—can lead to defensive and hurtful words. Taking a moment to breathe and collect your thoughts helps you respond with grace rather than emotion.

A.W. Tozer, in his Five Spiritual Vows, offers powerful insights for cultivating godly attitudes in relationships:

- *Never gossip.* Never pass on anything about anyone that will hurt them.

- *Never own anything.* Whatever we possess can end up possessing us.

- *Deal thoroughly with sin.* Confess your sins to God and

others. Make restitution where possible. Don't take the bait of Satan by holding onto offense—release unforgiveness.

- *Never accept any glory.* All glory belongs to God. Clinging to human praise can lead to pride and, ultimately, sin.

- *Never defend yourself.* God is your defender. If you are right, He will protect you. If you are wrong, admit it, ask for forgiveness, and make it right.

2. Clarify by Repeating What You Heard

When conflict arises, don't assume you understand. Instead, repeat back what your wife said to ensure you've heard her correctly. This shows you're actively listening and seeking to understand, not just waiting to respond. You could say: "What I hear you saying is..."

This practice slows down the conversation and gives you time to thoughtfully consider your response instead of reacting emotionally.

3. Understand the Goal of Criticism

If your wife's words seem negative or critical, pause and consider why. Reflect on your own actions—did something you say or do cause her frustration or hurt? Is she expressing pain from another situation that's affecting her emotions now?

Ask yourself:

- Is her comment constructive or simply emotional?
- Is she trying to hurt me or express something deeper?

Remember, "A gentle answer turns away wrath, but a harsh word stirs up anger" (Proverbs 15:1, NIV). Responding with gentleness can deescalate tension and lead to resolution.

4. Leave Negative Emotions at the Door

This doesn't mean suppressing feelings but choosing not to let anger or frustration drive the conversation. Instead, approach communication with love, kindness, and gentleness—the fruit of the Spirit (Galatians 5:22-23).

Negative emotions cloud judgment, but love brings clarity. Choose words that heal, not harm.

5. Own Your Responsibility

Use "I" statements instead of "you" statements. For example:

> *"I felt hurt when..."* rather than
> *"You always make me feel..."*

Owning your feelings fosters healthy dialogue, while blaming leads to defensiveness and disconnection.

6. Consider the Root of Criticism

Criticism is often a reaction to something deeper. Ask yourself:

- Is she reacting to something I said or did?
- Is she overwhelmed by something else, and I'm seeing the overflow of that stress?
- Is this a current issue or a resurfacing past hurt?

Understanding the source of criticism helps you respond with empathy rather than defensiveness.

7. Love Chooses Understanding Over Defensiveness

A man who truly loves a woman is not quick to defend himself but is eager to understand and resolve conflict with love and humility.

When you pause to breathe, listen, clarify, and respond with grace, you protect your marriage from unnecessary harm. Defensiveness builds walls—but love, patience, and understanding tear those walls down and build deeper connection.

Choose *connection* over defense.
Choose *love* over pride.

Guard Your Tongue And Her Heart

When a man really loves a woman, he guards his tongue and his woman's heart. It's impossible to overemphasize this important truth.

Jesus says that He only says and does what the Father tells him. A man should always be careful how he communicates with the one whom he really loves. While guarding his tongue, he is also systematically guarding her heart.

The Bible says:

 Husbands, love your wives and do not be bitter toward them.

— Colossians 3:19

I believe God knew how harsh men could be at times, so He specifically stated that men should not be punitive and severe.

* * *

Paying attention to the small details in your marriage lays the foundation for deeper trust and emotional connection. However, recognizing what makes your wife feel loved is only part of the equation. The next step is learning how to communicate effectively—openly, honestly, and with compassion.

In the next chapter, we'll explore how to strengthen your bond through intentional communication. You'll discover how to express your thoughts with clarity, listen to understand—not just to respond— and resolve conflicts with grace.

HOW TO COMMUNICATE
EFFECTIVELY

Every marriage will face moments of conflict, but how couples handle those moments determines whether their relationship grows stronger or begins to break down. I know this firsthand.

In the early years of my marriage to Kim, we often had what we jokingly called "heated fellowships." These weren't just small disagreements—they were full-blown arguments rooted in unmet expectations and misunderstandings. Looking back, I realize that much of our conflict came from how differently we were raised.

In my household growing up, my mother managed the home in specific ways. Naturally, I assumed Kim would approach household responsibilities the same way. But Kim didn't grow up with the same structure or expectations. Our assumptions clashed, and instead of discussing these differences openly, we let them fuel frustration and resentment.

It took time—and many of those "heated fellowships"—for me to realize that our real issue wasn't about chores or responsibilities. It was about communication. We didn't know how to express our needs or how to listen to each other with understanding.

That realization changed everything.

Once Kim and I began to focus on truly listening and communicating with each other, we found new ways to resolve conflict and build a stronger connection. We learned that communication isn't just about talking—it's about understanding. It's about paying attention to both words and actions, and responding with love and grace.

Follow the Rules of Heated Fellowships

When a really loves a woman, he is intentional about how he speaks to his woman when he's upset. Communication is the heart of marriage. When you master how to listen, speak, and understand, you lay the foundation for a relationship that can withstand anything. We developed a set of rules that helped us navigate "heated" moments. These simple, yet powerful principles allowed us to move from conflict to connection:

- *Be quick to listen, slow to speak, and slow to anger (James 1:19).* Prioritize listening over speaking and control your emotions. A calm heart creates space for understanding.

- *Be sensitive to verbal and non-verbal communication.* Pay close attention to not just what your wife says, but also what she doesn't say. Her body language, tone, and expressions can reveal deeper emotions.

- *No interrupting.* Allow your spouse to fully express her thoughts without cutting her off. Listening without interruption shows respect and helps you truly understand her perspective.

- *Control your emotions.* Don't let frustration or anger dictate your responses. Stay calm, even when the conversation gets difficult.

- *Watch your body language.* Non-verbal cues like crossed arms, eye-rolling, or dismissive gestures can escalate tension. Stay open and approachable.

- *Maintain eye contact.* Looking your wife in the eyes communicates respect, attentiveness, and a willingness to connect.

- *Be quick to forgive.* Let go of grudges. Forgiveness keeps bitterness from taking root and allows love to thrive.

One of the hardest lessons I had to learn during our "heated fellowships" was the power of patience. I'll admit, patience has never been my strong suit. But after making plenty of mistakes, I realized that if I took a step back and tried to see things from Kim's perspective—not just my own—it could completely change how we resolved our issues.

Conflict doesn't always need a quick fix; sometimes, it needs quiet understanding. Patience allowed me to slow down and truly listen, which often led us to peaceful resolutions.

Ruth Bell Graham once said, "A happy marriage is the union of two good forgivers." That truth has been a cornerstone in our marriage. Through patience and forgiveness, Kim and I have been able to grow closer, heal past hurts, and strengthen our bond.

No marriage is free from conflict, but with patience, understanding, and a heart ready to forgive, every disagreement can become an opportunity for deeper connection.

Implement Positive Non-Verbal Communication

When a man really loves a woman, he works on having positive, non-verbal communication. Positive body language is a powerful form of non-verbal communication. It shows that we are positioning ourselves in a way that allows those with whom we are communicating to feel comfortable and at ease. Simple gestures, like a friendly nod, can foster connection, while negative gestures—such as cutting your eyes at someone—can create distance and discomfort. Facial expressions and posture make a tremendous difference in whether the other person feels they are being treated kindly or unkindly.

A man who truly loves a woman is consciously attentive to both his and her non-verbal communication. Let's start with the obvious: when having a serious discussion, it's best to be out of earshot of the children and to speak calmly, using "I" statements instead of accusatory "you" statements.

Additional considerations are as follows:

1. *Eliminate Distractions.* Turn off all devices. I've noticed when Kim and I go out for a meal, many couples sit at the table completely disengaged from each other. It's as if the other person isn't even there. They're on their smartphones instead of listening and sharing face-to-face. At home, turn off the phone, television, computers, and iPads during important conversations.

2. *Sit Face-to-Face.* Look at and listen to one another. Avoid crossing your arms or legs in ways that physically close you off from your spouse. Instead, look at each other with an attentive and kind gaze.

3. *Hold Hands.* Holding hands can be a powerful, loving gesture during communication. While dating, it feels natural to hold hands. The same loving gesture can foster closeness and understanding during serious conversations in marriage.

4. *Listen Without Interrupting.* Focus on what's being said and avoid interrupting. You can show you're listening by responding with clarifying questions like, *"What I heard you say was _____. Is that correct?"*

Paying attention to your body language and creating a safe, focused space for communication builds trust and deepens emotional intimacy.

Do Not Interrupt

When a man really loves a woman, he listens without interruption. One of the most valuable skills a man can develop in marriage is the ability to listen attentively—without interrupting. Active listening is more than just hearing words; it's about being fully present and engaged in what your wife is saying. It shows her that her thoughts, feelings, and concerns truly matter.

Interrupting sends the message that what you have to say is more important, which can make your wife feel unheard or dismissed. In contrast, listening patiently and attentively fosters trust, respect, and emotional safety in your marriage.

Jack Nollan, in his article "How To Stop Interrupting People: 9 No-Nonsense Tips," outlines practical ways to become a better listener:

1. Practice active listening.
Focus entirely on what your wife is saying—without distractions. Maintain eye contact and lean in to show you are engaged.

2. Pause for 10 seconds before speaking.
Give yourself a moment to process what was said before responding. This ensures thoughtful communication instead of a quick reaction.

3. Purse your lips or cover your mouth.
A subtle physical reminder to stop yourself from interrupting.

4. Reflect back what you heard.
Use phrases like, *"What I hear you saying is…"* to confirm you understand her point. This shows you are listening to understand, not just to respond.

5. Let her continue if you interrupt.
If you accidentally interrupt, stop immediately and say, *"I'm sorry—please continue."*

6. Take notes (when appropriate).
In important conversations, jotting down thoughts can help you remember key points and prevent interrupting.

7. Acknowledge when you interrupt.
If you interrupt, own it. Apologize and allow her to finish speaking.

8. Ask a friend to hold you accountable.
If interrupting is a habit, invite someone you trust to gently correct you when it happens.

9. Practice with a partner.
Make intentional listening a regular practice in your marriage. Take turns sharing and responding without interruptions.

By mastering these habits, you create space for your wife to feel valued and heard. Active listening strengthens the emotional connection in your marriage and fosters deeper trust.

Create a Space for Meaningful Communication

When a man really loves a woman, he will create an atmosphere where his woman can feel free to share what's on her heart. She should know that her feelings matter to you and that you're eager to listen and understand.

This kind of open communication requires intentional effort. Regularly discussing both of your needs—*his needs* and *her needs*—can only happen when you prioritize intimate, meaningful conversations.

Make it a daily practice to:

- Spend time together in prayer
- Share Scripture and spiritual insights
- Engage in heart-to-heart conversations

Talking about the kids, finances, or work is important, but it should never replace the intimate conversations that deepen your emotional and spiritual connection.

Because of the love I have for Kim, I want her to feel comfortable telling me when something is wrong. We must resist the habit of saying, "Nothing is wrong" when hurt, misunderstanding, or conflict lingers beneath the surface.

Men are often "fixers." We instinctively want to solve problems and move forward. But loving your wife well means not only fixing what's broken around the house, but also repairing words and actions that fail to convey love, kindness, and understanding.

A man who truly loves a woman willingly steps into "fix-it mode" when it comes to resolving conflict and healing emotional wounds. This doesn't mean controlling the situation, but humbly seeking resolution through love, patience, and grace. He listens to understand, speaks with compassion, and leads with humility. In doing so, he strengthens the foundation of trust, respect, and love in his marriage.

IMPLEMENT THE 5 C's OF HEALTHY COMMUNICATION

When a man really loves a woman, he will create a loving and supportive environment that fosters intimacy. Praying and studying Scripture evoke intimate conversations. However, certain behaviors can become obstacles to building trust and fostering intimacy. These barriers include making demands, being disrespectful, expressing explosive anger instead of calmly speaking the truth in love, dwelling on past failures and mistakes, and resorting to blame or defensiveness. To cultivate a loving and supportive environment, practice *The 5 C's of Affirming and Positive Communication*:

1. Consistency:

When decisions are made, avoid changing them without intentional discussion and thoughtful problem-solving. Kim and I spend time together in the mornings in the Word and prayer to initiate consistent, intimate conversation.

2. Caring:

Positive communication should reflect deep care and affection in both words and tone.

3. Continual:

Intimate communication is a daily practice. Scripture counsels us not to go to bed angry. Be constant in your communication, both in good times and challenging ones.

4. Confronting:

Instead of avoiding issues, address them head-on without blaming your spouse. Speak the truth in love and take responsibility for your own feelings. Never say, *"You make me angry"* or *"You make me sad."* We choose how we feel. Use "I" messages instead of "You" messages to foster healthier dialogue.

5. Covenantal:

Remember that God surrounds you both and dwells within you. He is present in every conversation. Speak life, not death. Consider what God would say and what He would want you to do. Avoid intimidation, domination, and manipulation when communicating with one another.

By practicing these five principles, you can build a marital foundation of trust, understanding, and lasting intimacy in your marriage.

Communicate Better in Your Relationship

When a man really loves a woman, he will work on communicating more effectively. For more effective dialogue in your relationship, consider the five ways to communicate:

1. Ask Open-Ended Questions

Engage in meaningful conversations by asking questions that encourage your spouse to share their thoughts and feelings. Instead of asking yes-or-no questions, try asking, *"How did that*

make you feel?" or *"What do you think we should do about this?"*
This invites deeper dialogue and helps you better understand
each other.

2. Pick Up on Nonverbal Cues

Pay close attention to your spouse's body language, facial
expressions, and tone of voice. Often, what isn't said can reveal
more than words. Noticing subtle cues allows you to respond
with care and understanding.

3. Don't Try to Read Their Mind

Assumptions create misunderstandings. If something seems off,
ask rather than assume. Clear, honest communication prevents
confusion and helps both of you feel heard and valued.

4. Conversations Are a Two-Way Street

Healthy communication requires both speaking and listening.
Make sure you're not dominating the conversation or interrupting. Give your spouse space to share, and actively listen to what
they're saying without formulating your response too soon.

5. Set Aside Time to Talk

Life gets busy, but intentional communication can't be rushed.
Set aside uninterrupted time to talk about your relationship,
dreams, and even challenges. Whether it's during a daily walk,
after dinner, or a scheduled date night, consistent check-ins
strengthen your bond.

Bonus Tip: Be Clear About What You Need

Don't expect your spouse to read your mind. If you need something, ask for it directly. Expressing your needs openly can prevent misunderstandings and unnecessary conflict. Clear communication fosters mutual understanding and support, making it easier to navigate challenges together.

By practicing these simple yet powerful communication habits, you can create a stronger, healthier, and more connected marriage.

Meet Her Daily Needs

When a man really loves a woman, he looks for ways to meet her needs daily and share his needs. Spouses are not mind readers. They must ask for what they need.

When a man truly loves a woman, he intentionally looks for ways to meet her needs every day—and openly shares his own. Spouses are not mind readers. If something is important, it must be communicated. Expressing needs and desires openly creates a healthy foundation for understanding and connection.

So, how does a man stay intentionally sensitive to how full or empty his beloved's "love bank" is? The answer is simple: *communication.*

Consistent and meaningful communication is essential to truly loving a woman and understanding whether her emotional and physical needs are being met. As emphasized in the previous sections, intimate communication ranks high among a woman's core needs. A woman naturally desires to share her thoughts and feelings, while a man must become an engaged listener—fully present and unrestrained in conversation.

It's often said that women communicate more words daily than men. While this may be statistically true, it's not an excuse for disengagement. A man who deeply loves his wife must be intentional about engaging in conversations throughout the day. He should focus on a variety of topics—both lighthearted and meaningful—so he never misses what's truly important to the extraordinary woman he loves.

Even after more than 40 years of marriage, I continue to look for ways to meet Kim's needs. One simple way I do this is by going for early morning walks with her because she loves to walk. These walks give us another opportunity to connect, talk, and spend uninterrupted quality time together—one of her primary love languages.

It's the small, intentional actions and ongoing communication that keep love strong and a marriage thriving.

SPEAK BLESSINGS

When a man really loves a woman, he speaks blessings, not curses over her.

 Death and life are in the power of the tongue, and those who love it will eat its fruit.

— PROVERBS 18:21

We've all witnessed how some men can be harsh, hard, and unfeeling at times. This is why God clearly commands in Scripture:

 Husbands, love your wives and do not be bitter toward them.

— COLOSSIANS 3:19

When a man truly loves a woman, it is absolutely vital that he consistently and intentionally speaks life over her. Words have power. They can either uplift or tear down, heal, or harm. A loving husband must choose words that encourage, affirm, and bless his wife. When he does this, his words become a source of life, strength, and encouragement. Speaking blessings over your wife isn't just about making her feel good—it's about honoring her, uplifting her spirit, and building a marriage that thrives on love, respect, and mutual admiration.

Let your words be a reflection of the love you have for her. Speak life. Speak love. Speak blessings.

Dr. Dennis Golden, in his book Golden Nuggets, poses a powerful question: "What are the eight most important words in the English language?"

His simple, yet profound answer is:

- *Please*
- *Thank You*
- *Forgive Me*
- *I Love You*

These words may seem small, but they carry immense weight in a relationship. Make it a daily habit to use these words with your spouse intentionally. They foster kindness, gratitude, humility, and love— essential ingredients for a strong and lasting marriage.

* * *

In the next chapter, we'll explore how to build on this foundation by creating emotional safety and trust—a critical piece in strengthening your marriage.

LESSON # 6

HOW TO CREATE EMOTIONAL SAFETY AND TRUST

Men are called to be the spiritual leaders or priests of their homes. Part of that priestly responsibility includes protecting the privacy of what is shared between husband and wife. Confidentiality is not optional; it is essential.

The woman you love should know she can trust you with her most sensitive and personal matters. When something is shared with you, it should be as if she has placed it in a secure safe—locked away and protected. As a husband, you should be regarded by your wife, family, friends, and colleagues as trustworthy.

The Word of God reminds us,

 A talebearer reveals secrets, But he who is of a faithful spirit conceals a matter.

— PROVERBS 11:13

Respect Her as Your Best Friend

When a man really loves a woman, he respects her as his best friend.
While a wife may have close friends she confides in about certain things,
there are matters shared between husband and wife that are sacred and
meant for them alone.

Likewise, some things a man shares with the woman he loves are for
prayer purposes only. She must be able to hold those matters close and
keep them there.

Men also need to trust their wives' instincts and intuition. Women
often perceive things that men may overlook—subtle comments, body
language, or behavior from others that could signal inappropriate intentions. A man who honors his woman will listen to and trust the discernment God has given her, while also valuing her spiritual insight.

The Word of God says:

> Two are better than one, Because they have a good reward
> for their labor. For if they fall, one will lift up his
> companion. But woe to him who is alone when he falls,
> For he has no one to help him up!
>
> — Ecclesiastes 4:9-10

Do Not Dump On Her

*When a man really loves a woman, he refuses to dump his emotional
garbage on his wife.* Emotional garbage—or baggage—often stems from
unresolved psychological trauma, such as stress, trust issues, fears, and
other discouragements. These unresolved issues should not be placed on
the shoulders of the woman you love. Instead, men should be intentional about healing and working through personal struggles to become
the best version of themselves for their wives.

Your wife should never be treated as a dumping station for your
emotional burdens. She should be a refueling station, a source of peace
and restoration. Just as you should be deliberate about refueling and

uplifting her, she should feel safe doing the same for you. A dumping ground is where unwanted things are discarded—and that's not how the woman you love should ever feel.

Marriage comes with its share of life challenges, heartaches, and difficult seasons. However, your relationship with your wife should provide the opposite experience. It should be a place of healing, restoration, and peace—a sanctuary, not a landfill for unresolved pain.

When a man truly loves a woman, he protects her heart by handling his emotional struggles responsibly and nurturing a safe, supportive, and loving environment.

MAKE HER FEEL SECURE

When a man really loves a woman, he will make sure she feels secure in their relationship. A man must give the woman he loves every reason to trust the God in him. A woman typically desires security in a relationship above all else.

> *Make it your goal to create a marriage that feels like it's the safest place on earth.*
>
> — GARY SMALLEY

Security in marriage is built on a man being responsible, faithful, trustworthy, and dependable. Let's unpack these foundational components of a secure and loving covenant relationship.

1. Responsibility

Responsibility means responding in both word and deed with love, kindness, and positivity. It also means taking full ownership of mistakes, broken promises, or hurtful actions—without making excuses.

Responsibility requires transparency—being honest and coming clean. Transparency can feel risky because it means revealing your deepest struggles, fears, and mistakes. Yet, the reward of transparency is a deeper love and intimacy.

Transparency invites your spouse to truly know you—your strengths, weaknesses, dreams, and struggles. It says, "Into me, see." Without transparency, a marriage lacks the foundation of close friendship and trust.

A man who truly loves a woman practices ongoing and immediate responsibility, showing himself to be trustworthy. Transparency in a relationship is deeply attractive to women because it signals openness, honesty, and security.

When a man lives openly, without hidden agendas, it fosters an environment of trust and intimacy. Lack of transparency often indicates hidden sin, guilt, or shame, which builds walls of mistrust.

Ultimately, a man who truly loves a woman allows the truth of Christ to shine through his words and actions. His integrity is evident in his honesty, authenticity, and follow-through. Jesus prayed:

> Sanctify them by Your truth. Your word is truth.
>
> — JOHN 17:17

Integrity means doing what you commit to and communicating openly if circumstances change. A man of integrity aligns his actions with his words.

2. Faithful

Faithfulness is about being stable and constant. It begins with honoring marriage vows, maintaining moral purity, and avoiding anything that could harm the relationship—like pornography or inappropriate relationships.

My wife loves knowing that I will always be there for her. Despite our busy lives, she can count on me to prioritize our date nights, daily prayer and conversations, and celebrating special moments like birthdays and anniversaries.

Faithfulness is not just about physical presence; it's about being emotionally and spiritually present. It's a fruit of the Spirit (Galatians 5:22-23) that enables a man to sustain a trusting relationship with God and his wife.

Faithfulness means keeping promises, staying truthful, and being open about thoughts and feelings. It builds a foundation of trust that strengthens the marriage.

3. Trustworthy

A man who truly loves a woman must be worthy of her trust. This trust is earned through consistent moral, sexual, financial, and spiritual discipline.

Trustworthiness is built through dependability and promise-keeping. It's a quality that divorce-proofs a marriage.

I once heard a heartbroken wife say in counseling, "I don't think I can ever trust him again." In that moment, I realized: *Love is a gift, but trust must be earned.*

Trust is built through actions, not just words. If a man promises to be home at a certain time and doesn't show up, trust begins to erode. If he commits to completing a task and forgets, it weakens trust. Trustworthiness is demonstrated by keeping promises.

A woman longs to believe the best about her husband. She wants to feel secure knowing his intentions are always good and honorable.

A man who truly loves a woman ensures his yes means yes, and his no means no (Matthew 5:37). His words and actions align, showing reliability and dependability.

When trust is broken, a loving woman may choose to trust again —but it takes effort. Rebuilding trust can be challenging, but it's essential for intimacy.

Every act of trust risks hurt, but trusting love overcomes the fear of being hurt. Rebuilding trust starts with forgiveness, requesting truthfulness, and choosing to move forward in faith, not fear.

> There is no fear in love; but perfect love casts out fear, because fear involves torment. But he who fears has not been made perfect in love.
>
> — 1 John 4:18

When trust is broken, it must be intentionally rebuilt through repentance. This includes admitting the mistake without excuses, sincerely apologizing, seeking forgiveness, taking concrete steps to correct the wrong, and showing through consistent actions, that the mistake won't be repeated.

Trust can be rebuilt, but it requires intentional effort and patience from both partners. We will delve deeper into this topic in Chapter 10, where we focus on the practice of forgiveness and power of repentance.

Be Her Comfort

When a man really loves a woman, he comforts her in times of grief, depression, and despair. It is vitally important to show up when we truly love a woman—especially during times of grief, depression, and despair. In these vulnerable seasons, our presence and support speak louder than words.

Use comforting words like:

- "I am thinking of you and praying for you."
- "I'm sending you a warm hug."

Or, simply hold her in your arms without saying anything at all. Sometimes, silent support is the most powerful comfort you can give.

Ultimately, we need to show up 200% when the woman we love is in need. Proverbs 3:27 reminds us:

> Do not withhold good from those to whom it is due, when it is in the power of your hand to do so.

> — PROVERBS 3:27

As men who love our wives, we must offer everything within our power to support them in their most difficult moments.

I recently read a powerful quote in *I Love Myself, Do You?*:

> "If someone stays by your side through your
> worst times, they're the ones who deserve to
> be with you through your best times."

Let that be the standard we live by—standing strong beside the woman we love, through every season.

DECLARE YOUR LOVE DAILY

When a man really loves a woman, he will declare his love regularly. As you continue to invest in your marriage, begin each day by reminding yourself and declaring to your wife—the kind of love you are committed to:

"My love for you is patient and kind.
My love for you does not envy; it does not boast
*   and is not proud.*
My love for you is sacrificial and humble.
My love for you is not rude or self-seeking.
My love for you is not easily provoked and keeps
*   no record of wrongs.*
My love for you does not rejoice in iniquity but
*   rejoices in the truth.*
My love for you always protects, always trusts,
*   always hopes, always endures.*
My love for you will never fail."

(Adapted from 1 Corinthians 13:4-8)

Do Not Get Easily Angered

When a man really loves a woman, he refuses to let impatience escalate into anger. How would you characterize your anger? Does it resemble an explosive grenade or a firecracker with a slow, burning fuse?

> So then, my beloved brethren, let every man be swift to hear, slow to speak, slow to wrath; for the wrath of man does not produce the righteousness of God.
>
> — James 1:19-21

Anger is a natural emotion that can be either positive or negative. Gary Smalley offers valuable insight on this:

> *"Anger is an emotion. Like all of our emotions,*
> *   there's nothing wrong with it in and of itself.*
> *   It's our human response to something that*
> *   occurs—or at least our perception of that*
> *   occurrence.*

In fact, some anger is good; we should get angry when we see an injustice or when someone is trying to violate our personal boundaries. In such cases, our anger motivates us to take appropriate action.

But after anger moves us to do something good, we can't afford to let it linger inside us. We must get it out. Anger is a good emotion when it gets us moving, but if we let it take root, we set ourselves up for a great deal of potential harm."

Most anger follows four distinct stages:

1. *Impatience and Annoyance* – Instead of being quick to listen, slow to speak, and slow to anger, we often rush to respond when someone says or does something hurtful. We become particularly annoyed when they continue behavior they once promised to change.

2. *Frustration and Discontent* – This stage occurs when we begin to believe the other person isn't going to change, repent, or stop their hurtful behavior.

3. *Disappointment and Hurt* – Unresolved frustration can lead to deep disappointment and lingering hurt, which may give way to resentment, bitterness, and offense.

4. *Hostility, Rage, and Conflict* – Like simmering coals, buried anger can flare up into raging conflict when provoked, resulting in emotional firestorms and heated arguments.

Gary Smalley wisely stated that "the number one enemy of love is unresolved anger." When a man truly loves a woman, he follows the biblical instruction in the Word:

Be angry, and do not sin": do not let the sun go down on your wrath... let all bitterness, wrath, anger, clamor, and evil speaking be put away from you, with all malice..

— Ephesians 4:26, 31

A man who genuinely loves his wife practices patience by being a thoughtful listener and a patient, sensitive responder. Below are some practical strategies adapted from Gary Smalley to help a loving husband release unresolved anger and foster peace.

1. Paraphrase to Understand: Define and accurately describe the issue. A loving husband paraphrases what his wife says to confirm understanding. For example:

- "What I hear you saying is that you felt hurt when I didn't call you after work. Is that correct?"

2. Reflect Her Feelings: A man who truly loves a woman is sensitive to her feelings and reflects them back to confirm understanding. This gives her space to clarify or confirm her emotions:

- "It sounds like you're feeling overwhelmed right now. Am I understanding that correctly?"

3. Describe Observed Behavior: Pay attention to non-verbal cues that may indicate anger or hurt. Gently acknowledge what you observe:

- "I notice your tone is sharp, and you seem upset. Can we talk about it?"
- "You've been quiet and distant. I sense something is bothering you. Can we work through it together?"
- "I see you're crossing your arms and turning away. I want to understand what's going on."

4. Ask the Right Questions and Listen Actively: Be willing to ask thoughtful, open-ended questions and truly listen to her responses. Sometimes, her first answer may not reveal the deeper issue. Ask these questions with patience and compassion:

- "What do you want for yourself?"
- "What are you feeling right now?"
- "What are you doing about it?"

After listening, gently guide her toward reflection with spiritual encouragement:

- "What does God want for you?"
- "What is God feeling about this situation?"
- "What does God want you to do next?"

Encourage her to take action by asking:

- "Will you do what God is asking you to do?"
- "When will you take that first step?"

5. Use "I" Statements, Not "You" Statements: Avoid blame and take responsibility for your own feelings. Express how you feel without accusing her:

- "I feel hurt when we don't communicate openly."
- "I feel distant when we don't spend quality time together."

This approach invites conversation rather than conflict and fosters mutual understanding.

6. Offer Support, Not Solutions: Men often want to "fix" problems, but sometimes your wife simply wants to be heard. Instead of offering solutions, ask:

- "How can I support you right now?"

This shows that you care about how she feels and are willing to walk through the situation together. When a man truly loves a woman, he commits to patience over anger, understanding over judgment, and support over control. By managing anger thoughtfully and intentionally, he protects the relationship from harm and nurtures a lasting, loving bond.

DO NOT IGNORE PROBLEMS

When a man really loves a woman, he refuses to procrastinate when problems or issues arise. I once heard someone say, "If you see it, say it." This powerful advice emphasizes the importance of addressing issues at the appropriate time rather than ignoring it. Many of us struggle with this, but when we recognize a problem, we must learn to confront it that same day.

Taking prompt action prevents issues from festering, growing into resentment, and damaging the relationship over time. Unresolved problems can easily escalate, leading to bitterness and disconnection. Addressing concerns with care and urgency protects the bond between a husband and wife.

Throughout this chapter, we have explored the importance of positive communication, active listening, and the vital role a man plays in understanding and meeting his wife's needs. Ephesians 5 teaches that husbands and wives must mutually submit to and serve one another. As the head of his marriage and family, a man who truly loves a woman must lead as a servant, following the example of Christ in every aspect of his life.

Such a man embraces the humility and servant-hearted leadership that Jesus modeled:

Let this mind be in you which was also in Christ Jesus, who, being in the form of God, did not consider it robbery to be equal with God, but made Himself of no reputation, taking the form of a bondservant, and coming in the likeness of men. And being found in appearance as a man, He humbled Himself and became obedient to the point of death, even the death of the cross.

— PHILIPPIANS 2:5-9

Jesus embodied this selfless attitude when He taught His disciples that:

Greater love has no one than this, than to lay down one's life for his friends.

— JOHN 15:13

A man who truly loves a woman becomes her best friend and greatest protector. Like the Secret Service shields the President, a loving husband is always ready to take a literal or figurative bullet for the woman he loves. His commitment to protecting and supporting her is unwavering.

When a man refuses to procrastinate in addressing issues and leads with a servant's heart, he fosters a relationship built on trust, security, and unconditional love.

VERBALIZE & SHOW YOUR LOVE REGULARLY

When a man really loves a woman, he will consistently cheer her on by telling and showing her that he loves her. Actions speak louder than words, but both are essential when a man really loves a woman! Consider the insights and impartations shared regarding how a man should think, feel, and act to express genuine love.

Therefore, to him who knows to do good and does not do it, to him it is sin.

— James 4:17

For a man to develop an effective attitude of love, he must align his thoughts, emotions, and actions:

Right Thought → Right Feeling → Right Action

For example, we previously explored the importance of being quick to listen, slow to speak, and slow to become angry because man's anger does not bring about the righteous life that God desires. Simply agreeing with this truth isn't enough. A loving man must also feel openness and patience when his wife speaks. Finally, he must take the correct action: truly listening without interrupting, patiently waiting for her to finish, and resisting the urge to respond with anger.

So, what does this look like for Kim and me? After over forty years of marriage, Kim feels my love daily through my actions and hears it in my words. I kiss her every day and never miss an opportunity to tell her, "I love you." I believe that words and actions must work together to fully express love.

In her article "How to Show Your Partner You Love Them," expert Rachel Varina outlines five ways to express love, effectively:

1. *Communicate With Words:* Tell her how much she means to you.
2. *Be an Active Listener:* Show genuine interest in what she shares.
3. *Show Affection Through Actions:* Physical touch, thoughtful gestures, and support.
4. *Create Meaningful Moments:* Plan special experiences together.
5. *Show Respect and Appreciation:* Acknowledge her efforts and value her presence.

A man who truly loves a woman will intentionally think, feel, and act in all five of these areas to honor both God and his spouse.

BE SENTIMENTAL AND CARING

When a man really loves a woman, he makes it a priority to be both sentimental and caring in their relationship. Genuine love is not afraid to be tender, vulnerable, and expressive. A strong man understands that expressing love through meaningful actions and words deepens the bond with his wife.

Being sentimental, romantic, and caring can include:

- Listening *closely* and attentively, valuing her words and feelings
- Making sacrifices for her happiness and well-being
- Showing vulnerability and trusting her with his emotions and thoughts
- Loving how she looks—even on her "challenging days"—because his love goes beyond appearances
- Being proud of her and not afraid to show it publicly and privately
- Fighting *for* her, standing up for her and protecting her emotionally, spiritually, and physically
- Fighting *with* her (in healthy ways), working through disagreements to strengthen their bond
- Treating her family and friends with genuine respect and kindness

As a wise man once said:

> *"Nobody cares how much you know until they*
> *know how much you care."*

> — THEODORE ROOSEVELT

A man who really loves a woman shows his strength, not by being distant or stoic, but by being tender, attentive, and caring. His love is visible in both grand gestures and small, thoughtful actions—every single day.

Keep Her Love Tank Full

A man who really loves a woman consistently invests in her emotional well-being. Love should flow continuously, filling her "Love Tank" so she feels secure, valued, and cherished.

Never underestimate the power of simple but essential words:

- Please
- Thank You
- Forgive Me
- I Love You

Be Dependable

When a man really loves a woman, he must be dependable. This means a woman can trust him based on his integrity and consistent track record of keeping promises. A dependable man is truthful, honorable, loyal, constant, and steadfast. He is not double-minded or constantly changing his mind. What he promises today, she can rely on tomorrow.

A loving man demonstrates his dependability in tangible ways:

- *Calling* when he's going to be late.
- *Checking in* with a phone call or text while traveling.
- *Admitting mistakes* instead of making excuses.
- *Respecting boundaries*, while rejecting the mindset that it's easier to ask for forgiveness than permission.

Dependability builds trust and security, showing a woman that she can always count on the man who really loves her.

* * *

Building a foundation of trust is only the beginning of a thriving, God-centered marriage. Trust and emotional safety set the stage for love to grow, but love itself must be active, intentional, and demonstrated daily

In the next part of this book, we will dive into what it means to truly live out love—not just in words, but in consistent, sacrificial actions that reflect God's design for marriage. From being a protector and encourager to putting your wife's needs first, we'll explore practical ways to ensure your love is felt, seen, and cherished every day.

PART THREE

LOVE IN ACTION

Love isn't just a feeling—it's a choice and a commitment demonstrated through daily actions. A man who truly loves a woman understands that love must be active, intentional, and sacrificial. It's not enough to say "I love you"; those words must be backed by consistent, meaningful actions that make a woman feel valued, secure, and cherished.

In this section, we will discuss how to a man actively demonstrates love that strengthens a marriage and honors God by exploring:

- What it means to *be a protector*
- How to *create a safe space* for his wife
- How to *intentionally put his wife's needs first*
- Ways to *affirm*, *encourage*, and *celebrate* his wife
- How to be her *most loyal supporter* in every season of life

HOW TO PROTECT AND COVER YOUR WIFE

O ne of a man's greatest responsibility in marriage is to create a safe and secure environment where his wife feels loved, valued, and protected. This protection goes beyond physical safety—it extends to her emotional, spiritual, and mental well-being. When a man really loves a woman, he becomes her shield, her covering, and her greatest defender in every aspect of life. He will always make certain that she is protected.

The Lord shall preserve you from all evil;
He shall preserve your soul.
The Lord shall preserve your going out
and your coming in from this time forth,
and even forevermore.

— PSALM 121:7-8

COVER HER IN PRAYER

When a man really loves a woman, he will commit to being her greatest spiritual protector through constant, intentional prayer. He will cover her daily in prayer, seeking God's guidance and meaningful protection over her life. One powerful way to do this is by praying Scripture over her life, specifically Psalm 91.

I encourage you to pray this version of Psalm 91 over your wife, daily:

> *Most High God, You are our dwelling place and*
> *our refuge. I beseech you to keep your promise*
> *that no harm will befall us, and no disaster*
> *will come near our family and home.*
>
> *Lord of Hosts, I ask you to command Your*
> *angelic armies to guard, guide, and protect*
> *my wife in all her ways. Instruct my wife's*
> *guardian angel to propel her over every*
> *obstacle and hindrance that blocks her path.*
>
> *When the enemy comes against her as a roaring*
> *lion and poisonous snake, crust his head with*
> *her heal as You promised.*

God's angels are ministering spirits sent to protect His people (Hebrews 1:14). But our prayers play a vital role in activating that divine protection. A man who loves his wife will pray without ceasing, understanding that prayer is a powerful spiritual covering over his family.

For Kim and me, prayer is the glue that holds us tightly to one another and to Christ. It's a daily priority on both of our calendars. We pray for God's guidance, His protection, and the ability to understand each other in every circumstance.

PROTECT HER FINANCIALLY

When a man really loves a woman, he will cover and protect her financially. Men must remember that they are married to their wife— not to their work. Too often, some men fall into workaholism, justifying their neglect of their wife and family with the excuse, "I'm working day and night to provide for my family." In these situations, a man's job becomes his mistress, robbing his wife and family of the time, affection, and attention they need from him.

Providing financially is important, but it should never come at the expense of emotional and relational connection. I firmly believe it is a man's responsibility to cover the financial needs of his family if he is physically and mentally capable. Personally, I hold to the belief that "a woman should work because she wants to, not because she has to." My bride has not worked outside the home in over 30 years, and that has been a decision rooted in my commitment to provide for our family.

In Genesis 2, we see God establish this principle. Before God gave Eve to Adam, He ensured Adam had meaningful work and his own place to tend. The Word of God states,

 Then the Lord God took the man and put him in the garden of Eden to tend and keep it.

— GENESIS 2:15

This verse reminds us that God designed men to work diligently and provide. A man who truly loves a woman embraces his role as a provider —not to gain wealth for its own sake but to create a secure and stable environment where his wife and family can thrive.

MANAGE YOUR RESOURCES WELL

When a man really loves a woman, he understands the importance of being a wise and responsible steward of both his time and finances. This responsibility isn't just about providing—it's about managing resources well to ensure long-term security and stability for his family.

One of the foundational financial principles I've learned comes from Dave Ramsey's teachings on financial stewardship. He emphasizes the importance of taking small, intentional steps toward financial freedom. These steps include:

1. Building a Starter Emergency Fund: Setting aside an initial safety net to handle unexpected expenses

2. Paying Off Debt (Except the Mortgage): Using the debt snowball method to eliminate debts one by one

3. Establishing a Fully Funded Emergency Fund: Saving three to six months' worth of living expenses for long-term security

Kim and I personally experienced the value of these principles. During the pandemic, we went through a season of over a year and a half without receiving a regular paycheck. Yet, by God's grace and through our financial preparation, we were sustained by the emergency savings we had built. That season tested us, but it also showed us how faithful stewardship can protect and provide during uncertain times.

Another cornerstone of our financial stewardship is *tithing.* Kim and I are unwavering in our commitment to tithing because we believe wholeheartedly in the biblical principles of sowing and reaping. We have witnessed firsthand how God honors our obedience to "bring the whole tithe into the storehouse" (Malachi 3:10).

We don't just believe in tithing—we live it and teach it. God has blessed us abundantly, not just with provision but with *overflowing blessings.* Scripture promises that when we are faithful in giving, "the Lord will open the windows of heaven and pour out so much blessing that there will not be room enough to store it" (Malachi 3:10). This isn't about seeking blessings for ourselves, but about honoring God and trusting Him to provide in ways beyond our understanding.

Being a good steward of time and finances means prioritizing what truly matters—loving our wives well, providing stability, and honoring God with all that we have.

Protect Her Reputation

When a man really loves a woman, he protects her good name. In Matthew 1:18-19, Joseph provides a powerful example of how a man should protect a woman's reputation. When Joseph learned that Mary was pregnant, he planned to quietly break off their engagement to spare her public disgrace. His actions reflected deep care and respect for her, even before he fully understood God's plan.

When a man really loves a woman, he defends her honor and protects her reputation without hesitation. If anyone speaks negatively about his wife or brings up something unkind in conversation, it is his responsibility to shut it down immediately. Negativity or gossip should be addressed firmly and boldly in the moment—there is no need to delay.

When a man truly loves a woman, he covers her with affirmation, honor, and respect. He safeguards her dignity in every setting— whether standing up for her in public or supporting her quietly in private. His words and actions consistently affirm her value, demonstrating consistent respect and love. There is no room in a covenant relationship for revenge or "payback" in words or actions.

The Word reminds us:

> Repay no one evil for evil. Have regard for good things in the sight of all men. If it is possible, as much as depends on you, live peaceably with all men.
>
> — ROMANS 12:17-18

In moments of conflict, it can be tempting to lash out or say something hurtful. A man might later say, "I didn't mean to say (or do) that." However, it's important to recognize that every word spoken and every action taken stems from a choice. Hurtful words or actions don't happen by accident—they come from intentional decisions.

When a man truly loves a woman, he takes full responsibility for his words and actions. He does not tear her down to prove a point or protect his ego. Instead, he chooses to uplift and protect her reputation, showing her and others that she is deeply valued.

When a man really loves a woman, he supports her growth and covers her during seasons of personal development. Just as soil covers a seed until it blooms, a man should lovingly cover and nurture his wife until her gifts and strengths fully blossom. His love, encouragement, and protection create a safe space for her to grow and thrive.

Pray this blessing over one another regularly...
(insert his or her name in the blanks)

The Lord bless you and keep _____;
The Lord make His face shine upon _____
And be gracious to _____;
The Lord lift up His countenance upon _____
And give _____ peace.

— NUMBERS 6:24-26

COMFORT HER & HELP HER HEAL

When a man really loves a woman, he comforts her and helps to heal her hurts. A woman feels most secure when the man she loves actively comforts her, working diligently to relieve and heal anything that causes her pain. If it is within his power to remove or prevent something that could harm her emotionally, physically, or spiritually, he will step in to shield her. His love operates like radar, detecting and intercepting any incoming attacks—whether from human sources or spiritual forces—that seek to wound the woman he loves.

Comforting and healing her hurts means he covers her like a protective bandage, applying the soothing balm of his love and the healing power of Jehovah Rapha. His love creates a hedge of protection, ensuring that no further harm can reach her. This protective, nurturing love is beautifully reflected in *Song of Songs,* which serves as a biblical love manual for men who truly cherish their wives.

The beloved woman declares:

He brought me to the banqueting house,
And his banner over me was love.

— SONG OF SONGS 2:4-5

The Hebrew word for "banner" in this passage is the same word used for the military banners that Israel flew over their armies. These banners boldly declared to their enemies—both human and spiritual— that God, their Mighty Warrior, was with them, securing their victory and protection. God's banner of love shielded Israel, His beloved.

> The Lord your God in your midst,
> The Mighty One, will save;
> He will rejoice over you with gladness,
> He will quiet you with His love,
> He will rejoice over you with singing.
>
> — ZEPHANIAH 3:17

Just as God binds up the wounds of His people (Ezekiel 34:16), a godly man who truly loves a woman protects her and fights on her behalf. He stands against any force—seen or unseen—that would cause her harm. When she is wounded, he tenderly binds up her hurts with the *Balm of Gilead*— the healing, unconditional love of God flowing through him. He doesn't just stand beside her in the good times—he becomes a source of comfort, healing, and security in every season.

BE HER KNIGHT IN SHINING ARMOR

When a man really loves a woman, he will come to her rescue. Men, your beloved needs to know that you will show up for her—on time and fully present—as her knight in shining armor. Being dependable and arriving on time, whether for a date, an important event, or in moments of crisis, is like showing up on the battlefield for the love of your life. It's a powerful demonstration of love, commitment, and protection.

I remember years ago when my wife, Kim, was facing serious challenges at her job. The administration and her co-workers made the environment incredibly difficult. One day, she called me in distress, and without hesitation, I cleared my schedule, walked into her workplace, and retired my wife from that job right then and there.

In that moment, I told her she didn't have to endure another day of that toxic environment. She had the freedom to pack up her things and leave because her king had shown up, ensuring his queen would not have to tolerate such foolishness. Kim chose to walk out that day and never looked back.

As men, we must show up for our wives—not just physically, but emotionally, mentally, and spiritually. God should never have to ask us, as He did Adam in Genesis, "Adam, where are you?" Our presence, protection, and leadership should always be felt in our homes.

As I previously stated, my personal philosophy has always been: "My wife should work because she wants to, not because she has to." Therefore, it is my responsibility to care for my queen in a royal and intentional way—daily, weekly, monthly, and for the rest of our lives.

When a man truly loves a woman, this level of commitment and protection isn't optional—it's the standard he should set for himself and the expectation she should confidently have of him.

Use Your Powerful Weapon to Defeat the Enemy

When a man really loves a woman, he will do whatever he can to fight and defeat the enemy that may be coming against them. A woman needs to know that the man who truly loves her will use every spiritual weapon available to fight off any enemy threatening their marriage covenant. When a man really loves a woman, she can trust that he will stop any conflict between them and immediately begin to intercede in prayer, breaking every stronghold of conflict, confusion, or division.

A woman must have full confidence that her husband is a trusted prayer warrior—constantly watching over her and "wailing" in persistent prayer. She should know that her faithful, interceding man is drawing on every spiritual weapon in his arsenal to prepare for and protect the one he loves.

So, what are these powerful, non-worldly weapons we have access to as heirs in God's family? They are:

- Truth
- Love

- Righteousness
- Faith-Filled Prayer

These are the weapons of our warfare. They are not carnal, not of the flesh, and not of the world—but they are *mighty*. These spiritual weapons have divine power to demolish strongholds, pull down anything that exalts itself against the knowledge of God, and take every thought captive in obedience to Christ (2 Corinthians 10:4-5). These weapons work together in harmony, and none can be separated from the others—they are all necessary for victory.

In intercession, a man declares:

- *God's truth* over his marriage and family
- *His love* for God and for his beloved
- *Righteousness* through obedience to God's guidance
- *Faith* in God's promises, trusting and obeying whatever God commands

When a man truly loves a woman, she must know that he is always ready, willing, and able to defend, protect, and cover her completely. She trusts that he has the mindset of Christ—the heart of a servant leader (Philippians 2). He prays with bold faith, agreeing with God's Word that "No weapon formed against them will prosper" (Isaiah 54:17). This kind of love is a shield, a covering, and a spiritual fortress—a love that fights fiercely and prays relentlessly.

Provide for Your Wife & Family

When a man loves a woman, he finds ways to provide for his wife and family's spiritual, emotional, intellectual, and physical needs. He will do whatever is necessary to care for and support his wife. There's an old saying: "A man's got to do what a man's got to do." This means a man must take responsibility and do what's required to achieve the goals and fulfill the needs of his family—no matter the challenges.

But if anyone does not provide for his own, and especially for those of his household, he has denied the faith and is worse than an unbeliever.

— 1 Timothy 5:8

A man who truly loves his wife should be capable of leading in meeting her *spiritual* and *emotional* needs because he maintains a personal relationship with God and seeks His guidance for clarity and direction. This connection with God empowers him to be sensitive and attentive to her heart.

In the same way, a loving husband must recognize and respond to his wife's *intellectual* and *physical* needs. This means actively identifying what she needs, prioritizing the right time to fulfill those needs, and taking deliberate action. Love is more than thought—it moves from *perception* to *implementation*.

The word "provide" is a verb— it requires action. A man who intentionally loves a woman is:

- *Disciplined* in managing his time, energy, and resources
- *Diligent* in understanding and meeting his family's needs
- *Hard-working* and *committed* to ensuring his wife and family are supported in every way

Providing for your family is not only about finances—it's about covering your wife and family, holistically. A man who loves deeply ensures that his household thrives spiritually, emotionally, intellectually, and physically.

Defend Her

When a man really loves a woman, he is her defender, not a prosecutor. He stands by her side, protecting and guarding her from any hurt, harm, or danger that he recognizes could threaten her well-being in any way.

He does not criticize or focus on his wife's faults. Instead, he intentionally pursues the positive and builds upon her strengths. His words and actions uplift, affirm, and empower her, creating a safe and supportive environment where she can thrive.

He chooses to protect, not prosecute—to encourage, not criticize—and to stand beside, not stand against the one he loves.

PROVIDE WITHOUT LIMITS

When a man really loves a woman, she should continually feel and know that her man will provide whatever is needed to care for her for the rest of her life! A man's love should have no limits when it comes to meeting the needs of his wife and family, as long as he keeps God first and his spouse second.

The Bible instructs:

> Husbands, likewise, dwell with them with understanding, giving honor to the wife, as to the weaker vessel, and as being heirs together of the grace of life, that your prayers may not be hindered.
>
> — 1 PETER 3:7

Men, we are called to *honor* women. To honor means to regard a woman with the utmost respect and to recognize her superior value. She is a person whose worth commands admiration and great esteem. Proverbs 31 beautifully describes this honor:

> Who can find a virtuous wife?
> *For her worth is far above rubies.*
> Strength and honor are her clothing;
> *She shall rejoice in time to come.*
> Her children rise up and call her blessed;
> *Her husband also, and he praises her:*
> 'Many daughters have done well,
> *But you excel them all.'*

Charm is deceitful and beauty is passing,
But a woman who fears the Lord, she shall be praised.

— Proverbs 31:10, 25, 28-30

A man who truly loves a woman ensures she feels honored, cherished, and fully supported in every area of life. His love reflects not only provision, but unwavering admiration and deep respect.

Be A Solution

When a man really loves a woman, he helps carry her burdens instead of being a burden. A man who truly loves a woman naturally steps into the role of a protector and provider. He instinctively wants to fix her problems and ease her burdens. His desire is to carry the weight of her struggles, not to add more weight to her life. A man in love wants to be her hero—her Superman. He wants her to look to him as a problem solver, someone she can trust to step in and take action when needed.

In my own marriage of over forty years, my wife knows without a doubt that if she brings a problem to me, I will immediately move into "fix-it mode." She doesn't need to tell me when or how to act because she knows I will respond swiftly, decisively, and effectively. That's the kind of security and support every woman deserves.

When a man really loves a woman, he seeks to be a solution—not a burden. However, no man is omniscient. It's important to recognize that even the most attentive husband cannot always anticipate every need. Some women might think, "After all these years, he should know what I need." But that's not always the case.

Communication is essential.

- Don't bury your needs or expect them to be read.
- Pray about your needs and openly express them to each other.
- Regularly ask for help when needed, especially when emotional or physical burdens start to weigh you down.

When a man is attentive, he notices when his wife's emotional bank is running low—even if she hasn't said anything directly. By being proactive and engaged, he can help refill her emotional reserves through love, support, and thoughtful action. A loving husband is a burden lifter, not a burden giver.

Protect Her Honor

When a man really loves a woman, he properly rebukes those who do not honor and respect her. A man who truly loves a woman will always ensure she is honored and respected. He will not tolerate anyone diminishing her worth or treating her with anything less than the dignity she deserves. A loving husband recognizes that his wife is the queen of his life, and he demands that others recognize and respect her as well.

I remember attending a banquet years ago where I was offered a seat at the head table, but they placed my wife at another table. I refused to sit down until they seated my queen beside me at the head table where she belonged. In that moment, I made it clear that my wife deserved the same honor and recognition as I did.

When a man truly loves a woman, he doesn't passively allow disrespect. He actively ensures that she is treated with the utmost respect in every setting. This commitment reflects the biblical principle of "submitting to one another in the fear of God." (Ephesians 5:21). Loving a woman means standing up for her— always.

* * *

As a man, when you are committed to protecting and covering your woman, you demonstrate love by creating a safe and secure environment where she feels valued and cherished. However, love doesn't stop at protection—it extends into selflessness. True love calls for a willingness to place her needs above your own, ensuring that she feels prioritized, respected, and deeply cared for.

In the next chapter, we'll explore what it means to prioritize your woman's needs, the importance of selflessness, and how this Christ-like love strengthens your marriage and deepens your connection.

LESSON # 8

HOW TO PRIORITIZE YOUR WIFE'S NEEDS ABOVE YOUR OWN

A wise saying reminds us: *God first, family second, work third—and all else follows.* Prioritizing means making something a prime concern, a matter of utmost importance. For a man who truly loves (agape) a woman, she becomes his highest priority after God. Jesus affirmed this in the two greatest commandments:

 And you shall love the Lord your God with all your heart, with all your soul, with all your mind, and with all your strength.' This is the first commandment. And the second, like it, is this: 'You shall love your neighbor as yourself.' There is no other commandment greater than these.

— MARK 12:30-31

When a man really loves a woman, he will prioritize his wife's needs above his own. When he does that, he naturally becomes more attractive to her. His selfless love draws her closer, and in turn, she becomes more inclined to meet his needs, as well. Scripture teaches this principle of sowing and reaping—when you invest in your wife's happiness, that love and care will often return to you.

He will actively demonstrate his investment in her through attentiveness, support, and intentional care. His daily actions will reassure her that she is his priority, and he willingly meets her needs with love, patience, and understanding. This kind of love creates a thriving, joyful, and secure marriage.

Make Her Your Priority

When a man really loves a woman, he makes her his priority through intentional care. Marriage thrives when a husband is intentional about making his wife a priority. Intentional love requires both thoughtful consideration and purposeful action. A man who truly loves his wife places God first and his wife second—nothing comes between God and the woman he has been entrusted to love and cherish.

In the busyness of daily life, it's easy to get overwhelmed by the endless "to-do" lists—whether at work, managing household tasks, spiritual disciplines (prayer, Bible study, worship, service), or personal activities (rest, hobbies, self-care). Amid these responsibilities, husbands must be vigilant not to let intentional love for their wives slip down the priority list.

Modern distractions, especially excessive time spent on devices, can easily erode the quality of a marriage. Dr. Gary Chapman's concept of the "5 Love Languages" emphasizes the significance of *quality time* as a key expression of love. This isn't accidental— it's intentional. Husbands must purposefully carve out daily, uninterrupted, face-to-face time with their wives to nurture their relationship.

For me, this means committing to two date nights every week. This consistent, intentional time together shows my wife that she is a top priority in my life. Being "intentionally intentional" means not just thinking about loving her—but actively planning and following through with actions that express that love.

True love isn't passive—it requires deliberate, thoughtful action. A man who really loves a woman will consistently meet her needs.

A loving husband must be intentional in knowing and doing:

- What makes her feel *loved*
- What makes her feel *safe*
- What makes her feel *supported*
- What makes her feel *encouraged*
- What helps her feel *relaxed*

The Word of God reminds us,

 For you, brethren, have been called to liberty; only do not use liberty as an opportunity for the flesh, but through love serve one another.

— GALATIANS 5:13

Intentional love means paying close attention to what brings your wife joy and comfort. I know exactly what Kim likes—and what she doesn't. I intentionally keep track of this because it matters to me. As I previously mentioned, I have a dedicated section in my iPad where I list all the restaurants Kim loves, and I also note the ones we've tried that she didn't enjoy, so I won't take her back there. That's being intentional.

Another way I prioritize her happiness is by recognizing her love for perfume. As I've previously mentioned, I carefully list every brand and scent she adores in my phone so I'm always prepared when choosing a thoughtful gift.

Intentionality also means embracing spontaneity when it matters. I remember one afternoon while we were out driving, I turned to Kim and said, "Let's go get a hotel." Without hesitation, that's exactly what we did. She loves spontaneity, and because I know this, I lean into those moments to make her feel loved and cherished.

When a man truly loves a woman, he doesn't leave her happiness to chance—he is intentional in every detail, ensuring she feels valued, loved, and prioritized.

Celebrate Important Moments

When a man really loves a woman, he prioritizes celebrating the important moments in her life. He makes it a priority to remember and celebrate the important dates in her life—birthdays, anniversaries, promotions, awards, and personal achievements. These moments matter because *she* matters. By being intentional about honoring these special occasions, a man shows his woman that her happiness and milestones are deeply valued.

I make it a point to keep a calendar to remember every significant date in Kim's life. Beyond that, I intentionally find ways to make every day special because I am blessed to spend my days with her. Prioritizing these celebrations includes:

- *Her Birthday:* Celebrate the gift of another year with her. It's a blessing to love and cherish her for another year of life.

- *Your Anniversary:* Honor the commitment you've made to love one another— *"One Day at a Time for a Lifetime!"*

- *Her Promotions and Achievements:* Rejoice in her successes with joy and excitement. Celebrate every accomplishment as a shared victory in your marriage.

The Word of God reminds us:

 A time to weep, And a time to laugh; A time to mourn, And a time to dance.

— Ecclesiastes 3:4

There is always time to celebrate and dance in the joy of life's moments together! I've learned firsthand how important it is to honor these moments. There were times when Kim and I agreed not to exchange Christmas gifts. Yet, she would surprise me with a gift, and I would stand there empty-handed. Even though I tried to explain that I followed our agreement, I realized how important it is to acknowledge every occasion—even with something as simple as a heartfelt card. When a man really loves a woman, he doesn't let important moments slip by. He plans, remembers, and celebrates, making sure she always feels loved, valued, and prioritized.

Anticipate & Meet Her Needs

When a man really loves a woman, he prioritizes anticipating and meeting her needs. He will make it a priority to study her deeply, understanding what makes her feel loved, secure, and supported. He is attentive enough to anticipate her needs—whether it's offering a listening ear, giving her space, or providing comfort through a warm hug. He doesn't wait for her to ask; he actively observes and responds with love and care.

Years ago, Robert Schuller encouraged believers to "find a need and meet it; find a hurt and heal it." This mindset is essential in a marriage.

As the Word of God instructs,

 Beloved, let us love one another...

— 1 John 4:7A

Dr. Willard F. Harley, Jr., in his bestselling book *His Needs, Her Needs: Building an Affair-Proof Marriage,* identified ten essential marital needs. Understanding and meeting these needs is a clear way for a man to prioritize his wife:

- Affection
- Sexual Fulfillment
- Conversation
- Recreational Companionship
- Honesty and Openness
- Attractiveness of Spouse
- Financial Support
- Domestic Support

- Family Commitment
- Admiration

Let's expound on five of her top needs:

1. Affection

For most women, affection symbolizes security, comfort, and approval. Simple gestures like hugs or kind words communicate, "I care about you. You are important to me. I'm here to support you." True affection focuses on her needs, not your own.

 Though I speak with the tongues of men and angels, but have not love, I have become sounding brass or a clanging cymbal.

— 1 Corinthians 13:1

2. Intimate Conversation

Women need meaningful conversations beyond surface-level talk. Dr. Harley's research shows couples need about 15 hours a week of deep, intentional conversation. This includes discussing dreams, memories, and resolving issues kindly and thoughtfully.

3. Total Trust (Honesty & Openness)

A woman needs to feel that her husband is trustworthy and loyal. This means being honest and transparent and avoiding behaviors that compromise trust, such as engaging in inappropriate conversations or consuming pornography.

 And the Lord God said, 'It is not good that man should be alone; I will make him a helper comparable to him.'

— Genesis 2:18

4. Financial Support

A woman needs the security of knowing her husband is financially responsible. This involves managing a balanced budget, saving, giving, and investing wisely.

5. Family Commitment

A woman needs to see that her husband is a committed and loving father. Ephesians 5 teaches mutual submission, where the husband leads with servant leadership, modeling godliness for his family.

In *The Father Connection,* Josh McDowell highlights key qualities of a godly father:

- Unconditional love and acceptance
- Purity and truthfulness
- Trustworthiness
- Comfort and support
- Being a safe refuge
- Friendship and forgiveness
- Respect and godly discipline

Men should evaluate these traits and strive to improve where necessary. Discussing these qualities with your wife fosters growth and understanding.

REMAIN FOCUSED ON HER

When a man really loves a woman, he is laser-focused on her, and not distracted by other women. While it's natural to glance at others, he doesn't let his eyes linger or his mind wander.

Therefore, he will:

- Stay attentive to her, avoiding distractions
- Accept that God has given him everything he needs in his wife
- Honor their covenant, while protecting their bond

Maintain Your Health

When a man really loves a woman, he will maintain himself for her. He must prioritize his own health and appearance as a way to honor his wife. This includes:

- Maintaining a healthy lifestyle
- Stewarding his physical body well
- Promoting healthy routines and habits

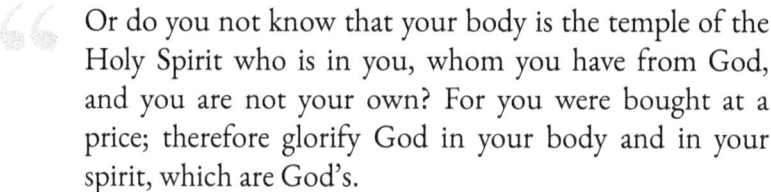

> Or do you not know that your body is the temple of the Holy Spirit who is in you, whom you have from God, and you are not your own? For you were bought at a price; therefore glorify God in your body and in your spirit, which are God's.

> — 1 Corinthians 6:19-20

A man's health allows him to be a reliable provider and an active, engaged partner. His physical well-being strengthens his ability to share in every aspect of life with his wife—from intimacy to enjoying activities together.

Value What Matters to Her

When a man really loves a woman, he values what matters most to her. If spending time with her adult children is important to her, then it should become a priority for the man who truly loves her. A loving husband recognizes how meaningful family connections are to his wife and actively creates opportunities for quality time together.

Family vacations often hold a special place in a woman's heart, especially when the children are growing up. However, many mothers still cherish spending intentional vacation time with their adult children and grandchildren. Knowing how much this means to my bride of over 40 years, I made it a point to plan a yearly family vacation every August. I personally handled all the arrangements and covered the costs. *Why?* Because it's important to her, and that makes it important to me.

Few things bring a woman more joy than seeing her family come together, sharing laughter and creating memories. As her husband, honoring this priority strengthens not only her happiness but also the bond within the entire family.

Some intentional ways to prioritize family time are:

- *Plan Monthly Family Outings:* If quality family time is important to the woman you love, organize a monthly gathering. This could be dining out, hosting a game night at home, or any activity that brings the family together.

- *Organize Summer Road Trips:* Arrange a family road trip to a new destination where everyone can explore, relax, and make lifelong memories.

- *Go on a Family Cruise:* Plan a cruise for the whole family, and capture the moments with plenty of photos. Share these joyful times on social media to celebrate a thriving, close-knit family.

According to the Word of God, there is a Biblical call to prioritize family. Scripture reveals:

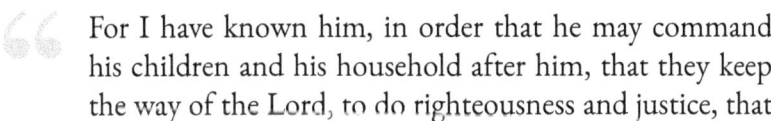
> For I have known him, in order that he may command his children and his household after him, that they keep the way of the Lord, to do righteousness and justice, that

the Lord may bring to Abraham what He has spoken to him.

— Genesis 18:19

This verse reminds us that God values the leadership of a man in guiding his family in righteousness and love. Prioritizing family time is not only a way to honor your wife, but also a reflection of God's design for a strong, unified household. He values what brings her joy and intentionally invests in creating meaningful family experiences.

Respect Her Priorities

When a man really loves a woman, he will respect her spiritual, physical, and emotional priorities. Loving her deeply means honoring every part of who she is. He understands that her well-being must be a priority in his life, second only to his relationship with God.

Respect Her Spiritual Needs

A woman's spiritual well-being is vital, and a loving man actively supports and nurtures her growth in this area. Here are some practical examples of how this can look:

- *Pray for Her and With Her Daily:* Consistent prayer strengthens the spiritual bond in marriage and invites God into every aspect of the relationship.

- *Stay Rooted in God's Word:* A man should study the Word of God regularly so he can pour into his wife from the spiritual overflow he receives.

- *Encourage Spiritual Environments:* He must ensure they both stay connected to spiritual communities that nurture their faith.

Some practical examples that we've implemented include:

- Hosting a *Couples Strengthening Couples* fellowship every month to invest in other marriages

- Serving on the *Board of Directors* for a marriage ministry called *Eusebeia*, where we participate in a spiritual revival for our marriage every year (Join us at *prayformarriage.com*)

Respect Her Physical Needs

A man who loves a woman also prioritizes her physical well-being by promoting a healthy lifestyle and fulfilling her physical and intimate needs.

- *Healthy Living:* Promote and practice healthy eating habits.
- *Physical Fitness:* Support and participate in regular exercise.
- *Intimacy:* Prioritize fulfilling her sexual needs and desires.

The Word of God provides Scriptural guidance on physical intimacy:

> The wife does not have authority over her own body, but the husband does. And likewise the husband does not have authority over his own body, but the wife does. Do not deprive one another except with consent for a time, that you may give yourselves to fasting and prayer; and come together again so that Satan does not tempt you because of your lack of self-control.
>
> — 1 CORINTHIANS 7:4-5

Respect Her Emotional Needs

Emotional support is critical in making a woman feel secure and loved. A man must prioritize her emotional well-being through attentiveness and care. Here are some practical examples of how this can look:

- *Keep Her Emotional Needs a Priority*: Pay attention to how she's feeling and respond with love and support.

- *Be Attentive to Emotional Cues*: Notice when she needs comfort, whether it's a hug, a listening ear, or simply your presence.

- *Be Present During Emotional Moments*: I personally know when my wife needs me to cancel everything, hold her close, and let her rest her head on my shoulder.

Make Her the Priority in Daily Life

Aside from God, nothing should take precedence over a man's wife. His time, energy, and affection should reflect her importance. Here are some practical examples of how this can look:

- *Daily Dinners Together:* We sit down to eat dinner together almost every night as part of our quality time.

- *Sleeping in the Same Bed:* My grandmother, Hattie B. Thornton (who lived to be 106 years old), once told my wife, *"Always go to bed when your husband goes to bed."* We honor that wisdom.

- *Two Weekly Date Nights*: These nights are non-negotiable and help us stay connected.

- *Quarterly Mini-Vacations:* We intentionally take short trips to unwind and reconnect.

- *"Just Because" Surprises*: I plan spontaneous events simply to remind her, *"Just because I love you!"*

When a man truly loves a woman, he naturally and joyfully prioritizes her needs—spiritual, physical, and emotional. He creates a life where she feels secure, loved, and deeply valued. Next to Jesus, the priority of a man's time, energy, and heart should be his wife.

BE SENSITIVE TO HER NEEDS & ACCEPT HER

When a man really loves a woman, he will be sensitive to her needs and accept her for who she is. A man's love for a woman is most powerful when it mirrors God's love—intentional, sacrificial, and unwavering.

Intentional love means being sensitive to your wife's needs before she even has to ask. It's a proactive, daily choice to love her in ways that resonate with her heart. A man who truly loves a woman doesn't wait for her to express what she needs—he studies her, knows her, and consistently shows up for her in meaningful ways.

Just as God intentionally loves and accepts us, a man must intentionally prioritize the needs of the woman he loves. This intentionality, fueled by time spent with God, allows him to understand her unique needs, put them above his own desires, and accept her for who God has created her to be. How accepting are you of your beloved?

 Therefore receive one another, just as Christ also received us, to the glory of God.

— ROMANS 15:7

To truly and authentically love a woman, a man must be intentionally sensitive to her needs—both spoken and unspoken. Let me explain what that looks like in practice.

When a man deeply accepts his wife, he naturally becomes attuned to her needs—physically, emotionally, mentally, and spiritually. He doesn't wait for her to express what she needs; he senses it because he is so connected to her. Here are some of the things he may be sensitive to:

- When she's overwhelmed and steps in to lighten her load
- When she needs comfort, a listening ear, or a warm embrace
- When she needs space and gives her time to recharge
- When she needs spiritual support or encouragement

This kind of attentiveness isn't accidental— it's the result of *intentional love and acceptance.* Acceptance is built on three foundational truths:

1. Acceptance Is a Choice, Not Just an Attraction

It is a deliberate choice, not merely a response to attraction. Attraction initially draws men to women in many ways— through physical beauty, personality, charm, chemistry, or even the scent of her favorite perfume. Emotional, intellectual, and spiritual qualities also capture attention. As we mature, we develop personal preferences, shaping the kind of person we're attracted to. But attraction alone does not sustain love.

Acceptance is far more powerful. It's a deliberate choice to love and embrace a woman for who she truly is, not for who a man wishes or imagines her to be.

Over the years, I've heard men in counseling say, "She's not the woman I married" or "She's changed into someone I don't like or love." These complaints reveal a misunderstanding of love and acceptance. The reality is that no one can change another person—we can only change ourselves.

When a man really loves a woman, he chooses to accept and love her as she is, through every season and stage of life. Initial attractions may fade or evolve, but intentional acceptance deepens love and fosters intimacy.

2. Acceptance Reflects Christ's Love

It mirrors the unconditional love of Christ. The command in Romans 15:7 to "accept one another" mirrors how Christ accepts us. The Greek word for acceptance, *proslambanō*, means "to receive, to take to oneself, to bring alongside." This is the kind of love a man must have for his wife.

When a man really loves a woman, he draws her close—not just physically, but emotionally, mentally, and spiritually. He invites her into his thoughts, feelings, plans, and decisions. She is included and embraced in every part of his life. This deep, intentional acceptance allows a man to become sensitive to her needs on every level.

The Word of God says,

> My beloved is mine, and I am his.
>
> — SONG OF SONGS 2:16A

This reflects the oneness marriage is meant to embody. Becoming "one flesh" means continually choosing to love, accept, and prioritize each other. It is an ongoing, intentional act of inviting and including your spouse in every aspect of life.

3. Love Reflects God's Design

Loving a woman well means fully accepting her as God created her. It's choosing daily to love her deeply, to prioritize her needs, and to protect her heart. This kind of love mirrors Christ's unconditional love for us—welcoming, inclusive, and sacrificial.

When a man really loves a woman, he doesn't wait for her to ask for what she needs. He studies her, learns her heart, and acts with sensitivity and care.

That is the power of intentional love.

 We love Him because He first loved us.

— 1 John 4:19

Understand Her Needs vs. Your Needs

When a man really loves a woman, he will prioritize her relational needs over his. As previously mentioned, Dr. Willard F. Harley, Jr., in his book *His Needs, Her Needs: Building an Affair-Proof Marriage,* offers valuable insight into how men and women differ in their relational needs. Recognizing these differences is key to loving a woman with intentional care. Let's compare the top five needs of women versus men.

Her top needs, include:

1. *Affection:* She needs to feel loved and cherished.
2. *Intimate Conversation:* She craves meaningful, heartfelt communication.
3. *Honesty and Openness:* She needs to trust him completely.
4. *Financial Support:* She wants to feel secure in their shared life.
5. *Family Commitment:* She needs him to be a devoted father and family man.

His top needs, include:

1. *Sexual Fulfillment:* Physical intimacy is vital to him.
2. *Recreational Companionship:* He enjoys sharing hobbies and activities.
3. *Physical Attractiveness:* He values his wife taking care of herself.
4. *Domestic Support:* He needs peace and order at home.
5. *Admiration:* He desires his wife's respect and appreciation.

Understanding and respecting these differences allow a man to love a woman in a way that deeply resonates with her heart. Consider reflecting on a personal experience I encountered with my wife, Kim.

There was a time in my life when I was earning a substantial income, and Kim could buy anything she wanted and travel anywhere she pleased. She even took trips with her friends without me. But one day, Kim came to me and said something that forever changed my perspective. She told me, "I don't want more money. I want you and our time together."

That moment made me realize that material things could never replace the value of quality time. Kim prioritized emotional connection over gifts and grand gestures. From that point on, I understood that intentional love requires consistent effort and presence.

CHECK IN REGULARLY

When a man really loves a woman, he knows the relationship requires ongoing, intentional effort. Love is dynamic and ever-changing, requiring a man to stay in tune with his wife's evolving needs. Regular check-ins should become a natural rhythm in the relationship— an intentional practice to remain connected.

- Ask her how she's feeling emotionally.
- Check in about her physical and spiritual well-being.
- Be attentive to shifts in her mood or demeanor.

By staying proactive, a man ensures he's never out of touch with his wife's heart. This attentiveness demonstrates genuine love and prevents emotional distance from growing.

Love suffers long and is kind; love does not envy; love does not parade itself, is not puffed up; does not behave rudely, does not seek its own, is not provoked, thinks no evil; does not rejoice in iniquity, but rejoices in the truth;

bears all things, believes all things, hopes all things, endures all things.

— 1 Corinthians 13:4-7

Biblical love is selfless and sacrificial. It prioritizes the needs of our beloved over personal desires. When a man commits to this kind of love, his wife will feel seen, valued, and deeply loved. This is the kind of love that transforms marriages and reflects the heart of God.

Serve Her

When a man really loves a woman, he is her earthly caregiver. One phrase that has always stuck with me is a wife proudly saying, "I'm not spoiled; my husband just loves me!" This statement reflects the heart of a man who genuinely prioritizes serving and caring for his wife.

A ministry colleague of mine, during his marriage seminars, often advises husbands to ask their wives daily, "How may I serve you today?" This simple, yet powerful question fosters a spirit of love, humility, and service in marriage. Scripture reminds us of this important principle:

 ...submitting to one another in the fear of God.

— Ephesians 5:21

A husband who truly loves his wife understands that serving her is not a burden but a joyful expression of Christlike love. He is her protector, provider, and most importantly, her partner in life, continually seeking ways to nurture, support, and uplift her.

Surprise Her

When a man really loves a woman, he finds joy in surprising her—especially if she enjoys spontaneity. Surprises are a meaningful way to express love and keep the relationship vibrant. Here are some creative ways to be spontaneous and show love:

- *Plan an Unexpected Trip:* Whisk her away for a weekend getaway or a spontaneous road trip.

- *Try New Date Ideas:* Explore creative date concepts like cooking classes, outdoor adventures, or themed nights at home.

- *Give Unanticipated Gifts:* Surprise her with thoughtful presents just because you can.

- *Break from Routine:* Take a break from your usual schedule to plan fun, unscheduled activities together.

- *Send Surprise Messages:* Leave unexpected love notes or send sweet text messages throughout the day.

- *Offer Random Gifts:* Small, thoughtful gifts like her favorite snack or flowers can brighten her day.

- *Show Random Acts of Affection:* Surprise her with spontaneous hugs, kisses, or holding her hand for no reason at all.

Kim loves spontaneity, so one year I surprised her with seven birthday cards leading up to her birthday. I hid each card in a different location, delighting her every time she discovered one. Small, thoughtful surprises like these deepen love and create lasting memories.

> *True love is inexhaustible. The more you give, the*
> *more you have.*
>
> — ANTOINE DE SAINT-EXUPÉRY

* * *

As a man, when you prioritize your wife's needs above your own, you reflect the selfless love that God calls husbands to embody in marriage. By making her feel valued, supported, and cherished, you lay the foundation for a thriving relationship. But prioritizing her needs is only the beginning. True love also means being her biggest encourager and unwavering source of support.

In the next chapter, we'll discuss how to champion your wife's dreams, celebrate her victories, and be the cheerleader she can always count on in every season of life.

HOW TO BE HER BIGGEST CHEERLEADER

One of the most powerful ways to strengthen your marriage is by being your wife's greatest cheerleader. When Kim feels led by God to pursue a vision or goal, I am the first to stand by her side. I support her emotionally, spiritually, and financially, ensuring she knows I believe in her. I consistently remind her of the calling God has placed on her life and speak life into her dreams.

Your words and actions carry the power to uplift and empower your wife. Be the man who reminds her of God's promises and encourages her to boldly pursue her God-given purpose. Your dedicated support can be the very thing that propels her forward into everything God has designed for her to achieve.

When a man really loves a woman, he intentionally uplifts her with words and actions. He becomes her encourager, strengthening and edifying her in all areas of life. In doing so, he reaps the blessings of a joyful, peaceful, and deeply loving relationship.

> Finally, brethren, farewell. Become complete. Be of good comfort, be of one mind, live in peace; and the God of love and peace will be with you.

— 2 CORINTHIANS 13:11

Focus On Her Best

When a man really loves a woman, he intentionally seeks out her best qualities and builds on her strengths, instead of spotlighting her weaknesses. Every person has both strengths and weaknesses, but in a loving relationship, the focus should be on encouraging and uplifting the one you love.

Rather than labeling her as "anal," recognize and celebrate that she is meticulous and detail-oriented—a focused, Type-A personality who ensures things are done with excellence. Instead of calling her "nosy," appreciate that she is naturally curious and engaged, which can help gather important information and keep things running smoothly.

A man who really loves a woman recognizes her unique qualities and supports her in thriving within her strengths. He becomes her biggest encourager, helping her grow and succeed in all areas of life.

 Therefore comfort each other and edify one another, just as you also are doing.

— 1 Thessalonians 5:11

Be Her Biggest Public & Private Supporter

When a man really loves a woman becomes her greatest source of encouragement, affirmation, and support. He is her biggest cheerleader—not just in private, but publicly. He openly celebrates her in front of family, friends, church members, neighbors, and colleagues. He actively rallies others to recognize and appreciate her strengths and achievements.

Dr. Gary Chapman, in his book *The 5 Love Languages*, emphasizes how essential words of affirmation are in expressing love and support:

"Words of affirmation are simply true statements affirming the worth of another person."

— Gary Chapman

No one should cheer on the woman in your life more than you. The term *cheerleader* is made up of two powerful words every man should embody when he truly loves a woman. He must "cheer" her on and be the "leader" in doing so. The word *cheer* means actively expressing applause or encouragement. Let's focus on the word *encourage*.

The New Testament instructs us 35 times to encourage one another. Paul commands it in *1 Thessalonians 5:11*: "Encourage one another and build each other up." The word *encourage* literally means to infuse or impart courage into someone.

One of the greatest human struggles is fear. A man who truly loves a woman helps cast out that fear. He empowers her to be bold and courageous because God has not given her a spirit of fear but of power, love, and a sound mind (2 Timothy 1:7).

My favorite synonym for encourager is *cheerleader*. A cheerleader is someone who actively infuses joy, strength, hope, and positivity into every word, action, and situation. He leads with encouragement, always ranking first in her support system.

The man who truly loves a woman is her most devoted fan, lifting her up through challenges and triumphs. He reminds her of her God-given strength, encouraging her to grow, develop, and thrive— always cheering her on to be her absolute best, regardless of who's around. He will honor and celebrate her both publicly and privately. His love and admiration are not hidden but expressed in intentional ways that make her feel valued, cherished, and secure.

Here are some ways you can publicly praise and celebrate a woman:

Speak Words of Affirmation in Public:

- Verbally express how much you love and appreciate her in front of family, friends, and even strangers.
- Compliment her achievements, character, and beauty in social settings.

Show Physical Affection:

- Hold her hand, wrap your arm around her, or let her hold your arm during a walk.
- These small gestures show the world she is loved, protected, and prioritized.

Offer Public Romantic Gestures:

- Surprise her with flowers at her office or home.
- Have her favorite chocolates delivered to her workplace with a sweet note.
- Give her a "Just Because" gift—not tied to any occasion—simply to say, "I love and adore you."

Here are some ways you can privately praise and celebrate a woman:

Surprise Thoughtful Gifts:

- Pay attention to the little things she admires or mentions and surprise her with them.
- Send her something special when she least expects it—a book she mentioned, a piece of jewelry she admired, or a cozy item for her comfort.

Personal Notes and Messages:

- Leave handwritten notes in places she'll find them—a mirror, her purse, or in her lunch.
- Send unexpected, heartfelt text messages during the day to let her know you're thinking about her.

Create Special Moments:

- Plan intimate, meaningful experiences just for the two of you—like a spontaneous dinner at home with her favorite meal or a relaxing evening watching her favorite movie.

Publicly honoring your wife shows the world how much she means to you, reinforcing her worth and value. Privately celebrating her nurtures intimacy and emotional security, reminding her she's cherished in every space you share.

When a man consistently praises the woman he loves—both publicly and privately—he builds a foundation of trust, love, and admiration that strengthens their bond.

ENCOURAGE INSTEAD OF DISCOURAGE

A man who really loves a woman is her constant source of encouragement, not criticism. He lifts her up, supports her dreams, and strengthens her spirit. Encouragement is more than kind words—it's an intentional act of love that empowers her to become all that God created her to be.

Consider the following five ways to encourage the woman you love. These ideas are adapted from "5 Ways to Encourage the Ones You Love," by Granite Wellness Centers.

1. Show Genuine Interest

- Ask thoughtful questions and actively listen.
- Show you care about her dreams, struggles, and victories.
- Be sincere and consistent in your interest.

2. Acknowledge What's Important to Her

- Validate her passions and pursuits.
- Celebrate what matters most to her, even if it's different from your own interests.

- Your affirmation boosts her confidence and self-esteem.

3. Say, "You're Doing a Great Job"

- Offer genuine praise for her hard work and accomplishments.
- Simple words like "Well done" or "I'm proud of you" can inspire her to keep going.

4. Say, "Thank You"

- Express gratitude for the everyday things she does.
- Whether it's cooking a meal or supporting you, acknowledge her efforts.

5. Offer to Lend a Hand

- Don't wait for her to ask—be proactive in offering help.
- Your willingness to invest time and energy shows deep care and commitment.

Let's explore the deeper biblical meaning of encouragement:

In Hebrew (*Chazaq*):

- To make strong, to strengthen
- To support and sustain
- To repair and restore
- To take hold of and prevail

In Deuteronomy 3:28, God commanded Moses to "charge Joshua, and encourage him, and strengthen him." Likewise, when a man really loves a woman, he is called to strengthen and sustain her through all seasons—both in better and worse times.

In Greek (*Oikodomoo*):

- To build up
- To edify
- To comfort and console

The Word of God reminds us:

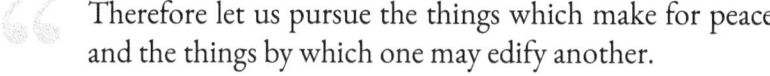

> Therefore let us pursue the things which make for peace and the things by which one may edify another.
>
> — ROMANS 14:19

> Again, do you think that we excuse ourselves to you? We speak before God in Christ. But we do all things, beloved, for your edification.
>
> — 2 CORINTHIANS 12:19

Encouragement means building her up—not tearing her down. A man who really loves his woman builds her up emotionally, spiritually, and mentally, guiding her through life's highs and lows with steadfast support.

The opposite of encouragement is criticism—a destructive force in any relationship. Harsh, negative words can tear down a woman's spirit and create emotional distance. A wise poet once said:

If a child lives with criticism, he learns to condemn.
If a child lives with hostility, he learns to fight.
If a child lives with ridicule, he learns to be shy.
If a child lives with shame, he learns to feel guilty.

Men of God, be mindful of your words. What you sow into your relationship, you will reap. Criticism breeds condemnation, but encouragement fosters love, joy, and peace.

NOTICE AND PRAISE THE LITTLE THINGS SHE DOES

When a man really loves a woman, he doesn't overlook the small, thoughtful things she does for him and their family; he acknowledges and celebrates them. Recognizing these everyday acts of love deepens the bond between them and reassures her that her efforts are seen, valued, and appreciated.

I often tell my wife, "I thank God for allowing me the privilege and pleasure of loving you!" God could have allowed her to be with anyone else, but I am beyond grateful for the honor of loving this incredible woman of God.

A man must never take the woman he loves for granted. He should express sincere appreciation for all she does, especially for the unseen sacrifices and quiet ways she serves and nurtures the family.

One of the most powerful and often overlooked love languages is *prayer.* If your wife is the intercessor for your home—praying faithfully for you, your children, and your family's well-being—that alone is a reason to praise and honor her. Prayer is one of the deepest forms of love, a spiritual act of carrying burdens and speaking blessings over the family.

Prayer is a powerful love language:

- *With God:* Prayer fosters a constant, intimate relationship with God, allowing us to seek His heart and guidance. Some believe that God uses prayer to draw people closer to His heart, wooing them into a deeper relationship with Him.

- *With Others:* Prayer is a profound way to show love and compassion for others. It's a selfless act of bearing someone else's burdens and standing in spiritual agreement for their good.

- *As an Expression of Love:* World Help describes prayer as one of the greatest acts of love because it allows us to lovingly intercede for others, lifting their needs and desires before God.

Imagine the impact of saying to your wife, "Thank you for praying for me. I feel covered and loved because of your prayers." Recognizing her spiritual labor not only honors her efforts but also encourages her to continue standing in faith for your family.

A man who really loves a woman should continually praise her for all the ways she serves in love—whether it's through prayer, nurturing the children, managing the home, or simply offering quiet support. Let her know you see her sacrifices. Let her know you value her love. Let her know that the little things she does mean everything to you.

* * *

Being your wife's biggest cheerleader means encouraging her to pursue her dreams, celebrating her strengths, and standing by her side through every challenge. It's a beautiful way to build trust, deepen intimacy, and show her she is truly cherished. But the greatest gift you can give her is cultivating a marriage grounded in faith.

In the next chapter, we'll explore how to strengthen your relationship by anchoring it in God's word and prioritizing spiritual growth together. A Christ-centered marriage is not only a source of joy, but also a powerful testimony of God's love.

PART FOUR

A CHRIST-CENTERED MARRIAGE

A Christ-centered marriage is the foundation for a strong, lasting, and fulfilling relationship. When Christ is at the center, love becomes deeper, communication grows stronger, and forgiveness becomes easier. This section focuses on how couples can invite God into every part of their marriage, allowing His love to guide their actions and decisions. It also explores the transformative power of forgiveness—an essential practice for maintaining unity, healing wounds, and strengthening the marital bond. By prioritizing spiritual growth and grace, couples can experience the fullness of God's design for marriage.

In this section, we will explore how to:

- Build a solid spiritual foundation
- Lead and serve each other in love
- Create spiritual routines that keep God at the center
- Understand the power of forgiveness
- Let go of past hurts and move forward in grace
- Reflect Christ's forgiveness by extending mercy

HOW TO CULTIVATE A SPIRITUALLY STRONG MARRIAGE

The foundation of a Christ-centered marriage begins with both husband and wife having a personal, growing relationship with Jesus Christ. Before entering a covenant marriage, both partners must be fully surrendered to God. As Romans 10:9 reminds us, confessing Jesus as Lord and believing in His resurrection is the cornerstone of a believer's faith.

> ...that if you confess with your mouth the Lord Jesus and believe in your heart that God has raised Him from the dead, you will be saved.
>
> — ROMANS 10:9

SUPPORT HER SPIRITUAL GROWTH

When a man really loves a woman, he will ensure that her spiritual needs are supported. In pre-marital counseling, the first and most critical conversation I have with couples is about their relationship with God. A man who truly loves a woman must be confident in making her *godly priorities* his own. This includes supporting her spiritual disciplines like prayer, Bible study, worship, service, giving, meditation, solitude with God, and fasting.

If she values quiet time with God, he should actively create space for her to nurture that relationship. Prioritizing her spiritual well-being demonstrates intentional love. By supporting her walk with God, he contributes to the spiritual foundation of their relationship and their shared growth in Christ.

Three practical ways to demonstrate that are:

1. Encourage Rest and Renewal: Give her "Do Nothing Days" or at least half-days weekly to refresh and avoid burnout. This not only supports her physical and emotional health but also creates an opportunity for her to spend uninterrupted time in prayer, Bible study, or meditation, deepening her spiritual connection with God.

2. Prioritize Weekly Date Nights: Take her out at least once a week to show her that her time and companionship are valued. This practice strengthens your bond as a couple, which is a reflection of God's design for marriage. A strong, loving relationship allows her to thrive spiritually, knowing she is loved and supported in an environment of mutual care and trust.

3. Plan Quarterly Getaways: Organize mini-vacations or staycations to break from routine and deepen your connection. These intentional breaks from daily life give both of you the chance to reconnect not only with each other but also with God. Sharing moments of gratitude and reflection together during these times can strengthen her faith and enrich your spiritual partnership.

By prioritizing her rest, quality time, and renewal, you're not just demonstrating love in action—you're actively supporting her spiritual journey.

Jesus modeled this balance:

 Now in the morning, having risen a long while before daylight, He went out and departed to a solitary place; and there He prayed.

— MARK 1:35

Therefore, couples should follow Christ's example, cultivating both individual and shared time with God. This benefits both her relationship with God and your covenant as a couple.

GROW IN GOD TOGETHER

When a man truly loves a woman, he prioritizes building a relationship firmly rooted in God. It's important to him that they are actively nurturing their spiritual connection so they can grow closer to Him together. Paul Stevens, in *Marriage Spirituality: Ten Disciplines for Couples Who Love God*, emphasizes intentional spiritual growth as a couple. He defines marriage spirituality as being deliberate about developing a relationship with God through Christ in response to His grace.

Stevens' Ten Spiritual Disciplines for Couples:

1. *Prayer*: Daily, consistent prayer as a couple
2. *Guided Conversations*: Purposeful talks about faith and life
3. *Sabbath Keeping*: Worship, rest, and spiritual reflection
4. *Shared Retreats for Solitude*: Time away to seek God
5. *Study*: Joint Bible study and learning.
6. *Service*: Serving God and others together
7. *Sexual Fasting*: Spiritual discipline for focused prayer (1 Corinthians 7:5)
8. *Obedience*: Acting on God's Word in daily life
9. *Confession*: Openly confessing sins to God and one another

10. *Mutual Submission:* Serving each other out of reverence for Christ (Ephesians 5:21)

Intentionality is key. Discipline requires planning and practicing faith, starting with prayer. As Scripture says, "Pray without ceasing" (1 Thessalonians 5:17).

By intentionally prioritizing God and each other, couples create a spiritually strong marriage that can withstand any challenge and flourish in God's grace.

PRAY TOGETHER WITHOUT CEASING

When a man really loves a woman, he will pray regularly with her. The saying is true: Couples and families that pray together stay together. Kim and I once committed to a 21-day fast at the end of the year to seek clarity and direction for our marriage. We constantly strive to strengthen our relationship in ways that allow our marriage to grow and thrive, rather than merely survive. That 21-day fast was truly transformative. Notice, I didn't say it was pleasurable—but it was absolutely amazing.

During the fast, we prayed regularly, as God revealed areas in both of us that needed to be addressed and prayed through. It wasn't always easy, but it was necessary. It reminded us that prayer works, and that some breakthroughs only happen through the intentional process of fasting and praying.

 However, this kind does not go out except by prayer and fasting.

— MATTHEW 17:21

Let prayer and fasting be a foundation in your marriage, drawing you closer to God and each other.

TEAR DOWN SPIRITUAL STRONGHOLDS TOGETHER

When a man really loves a woman, he builds an epic spiritual partnership designed to confront and destroy anything that threatens their marriage or relationship. He takes the lead spiritually, creating a solid foundation that exposes and dismantles any force working against their union.

He acts with the same vigilance and precision as a Secret Service agent protecting the President of the United States—constantly on guard to ensure that nothing tears down what God has created between them.

> For though we walk in the flesh, we do not war according to the flesh. For the weapons of our warfare are not carnal but mighty in God for pulling down strongholds, casting down arguments and every high thing that exalts itself against the knowledge of God, bringing every thought into captivity to the obedience of Christ.
>
> — 2 CORINTHIANS 10:3-5

Spiritual weapons help you:

1. Pull Down Strongholds:

Strongholds are deeply rooted offenses or past hurts that resurface during conflict, often magnifying current issues. Instead of addressing the present situation, past pain, guilt, and emotional baggage resurface, turning minor disagreements into major conflicts. These need to be intentionally identified and torn down.

2. Cast Down Arguments:

Repetitive arguments stem from unresolved issues. Even when

the situation changes, the same unhealthy patterns of disagreement emerge. Spiritually discerning these patterns allows couples to break the cycle of recurring conflict.

3. *Tear Down Every High Thing That Exalts Itself Against God:*

Emotional walls of hurt, pride, and offense block God's truth and wisdom from entering the relationship. When opinions and emotions take precedence over God's Word, they create division. A spiritually strong couple recognizes and dismantles these barriers, allowing God's truth to reign.

4. *Take Every Thought Captive to the Obedience of Christ:*

A man who loves a woman will align his thoughts—and encourage her to align hers—with God's truth rather than relying on feelings or personal desires. He prioritizes obedience to God's direction over personal reasoning or emotional reactions.

BUILD A SPIRITUAL SHIELD AROUND YOUR FAMILY

When a man really loves a woman, he becomes a spiritual warrior for their relationship. Together, they use God's powerful weapons—prayer, fasting, Scripture, forgiveness, and worship—to guard their marriage against spiritual attacks.

He is intentional about praying over generational curses, recognizing spiritual patterns that may have followed either family line, and breaking them in Jesus' name. He stands in the gap, leading his family with discernment, strength, and unwavering faith.

By leading with spiritual authority and love, a man not only protects his marriage but also ensures it thrives under God's covering.

PRAY OVER HER WITH BLESSINGS AND THANKSGIVING

When a man really loves a woman, she should always be at the top of his prayer list. I pray for my wife, Kimberely Reeder Allen, every single day because she is that important to me! My daily request is that God would grant the woman I love divine direction and divine protection every moment of every day. As her husband, I am responsible for covering the woman I love in prayer. Seeking God on her behalf means going directly to the Creator of Heaven and Earth to ask for His very best for her life.

The Bible instructs us:

> Be anxious for nothing, but in everything by prayer and supplication, with thanksgiving, let your requests be made known to God.
>
> — PHILIPPIANS 4:6

When a man really loves a woman, he saturates her in prayer— covering her with blessings, favor, and protection. She should feel completely drenched in God's love and care through the prayers of the man who loves her. He should deeply desire to give his beloved his absolute best— and the very best he can offer comes from the omnipresent, all-powerful God. There is no greater gift than lifting her up before the Lord, asking Him to guide her steps, strengthen her spirit, and surround her with His peace.

EQUIP HER WITH GOD'S WISDOM

When a man really loves a woman, he seeks God for the wisdom and guidance to love her unconditionally. There is no greater wisdom than the wisdom that comes directly from God! As a man pursues God for insight, knowledge, and truth, God empowers him—through His Word —to love on a deeper and more meaningful level.

The Word of God declares:

 Now to Him who is able to do exceedingly abundantly above all that we ask or think, according to the power that works in us, to Him be glory in the church by Christ Jesus to all generations, forever and ever. Amen.

— Ephesians 3:20-21

God grants wisdom beyond what we could ever ask or imagine. As men grow in this divine wisdom, they can pour it into the woman they love, equipping her to walk in spiritual strength and truth.

Scripture reminds us:

 For the word of God is living and powerful, and sharper than any two-edged sword, piercing even to the division of soul and spirit, and of joints and marrow, and is a discerner of the thoughts and intents of the heart.

— Hebrews 4:12

A man of God who really loves his woman will do his very best to connect her to God's Word because it is through Scripture that she will experience her greatest growth and spiritual maturity.

By sharing God's truth, praying with her, and guiding her toward God's promises, a man becomes a spiritual leader in their relationship. He encourages her to seek God, grounding their love in the unshakable foundation of His Word. This kind of love fosters a Christ-centered relationship where both partners grow stronger in faith and walk boldly in God's purpose for their lives.

Be Persistent in Pursuing God's Vision

When a man really loves a woman, he will be intentional about seeking God's vision for his marriage and family. The word *pursue* means to actively and intentionally employ measures to accomplish a specific task. In marriage, this means persistently seeking God's vision for a triumphant, victorious, and lasting relationship. A man who truly loves a woman must be patient and diligent in pursuing God's purpose for their marriage and family.

One crucial question I often ask God after reaching a milestone in life is, "What's next?" I am continually seeking God's direction for myself and my family. Beyond seeking, I share what God reveals with my wife and invite her input and prayers as we journey together. A marriage rooted in God requires both partners to actively pursue God and His vision for their union.

He must *pursue God first* and then lovingly pursue her. This pursuit is ongoing—through prayer, listening, Bible study, and intentional leadership—not through pressure but through gentle guidance. True leadership in marriage is built on consistently opening the door for communication with God and with his wife.

A triangle covenant is a visual diagram I use when working with couples. With God at the top and both partners positioned on either side, the illustration shows that as each person actively pursues God, they naturally grow closer to one another. Therefore, a man must constantly seek God's will concerning the woman he loves if he desires to be the best husband for God's glory and for his wife's joy.

By passionately pursuing God's vision, a loving man:

- *Prays for and with his wife* about their family's direction
- *Listens for God's guidance* and involves his wife in decision-making
- *Leads by example,* seeking God daily and encouraging his wife to do the same
- *Works together* with his wife to align their goals with God's will

A man who relentlessly chases after God's vision becomes a spiritual anchor in his home, creating a marriage and family built on faith, love, and God's divine purpose.

Ask For Her Support

When a man really loves a woman, he humbly acknowledges his need for the unique, God-ordained role she plays in his life. He recognizes that God created her to complete him and help him grow into the man of God he is destined to be.

God's Word beautifully illustrates this truth:

> And the Lord God caused a deep sleep to fall on Adam, and he slept; and He took one of his ribs, and closed up the flesh in its place. Then the rib which the Lord God had taken from man He made into a woman, and He brought her to the man.
>
> And Adam said:
>
> 'This is now bone of my bones
>   And flesh of my flesh;
>   She shall be called Woman,
>   Because she was taken out of Man.'
>
> — Genesis 2:21-23

A loving husband understands that God designed his wife to strengthen, support, and sharpen him. She is a queen who empowers him to mature spiritually, emotionally, and mentally. Her presence in his life is not by accident, but by divine design to help him become everything God has called him to be.

Moreover, he also recognizes the power of having a praying wife. He understands that her prayers have been instrumental in advancing his life and pushing him toward his God-given purpose. James 5:16 (NASB) reminds us that "the effective, fervent prayer of a righteous person has great power." Through her prayers, a righteous woman releases healing, comfort, forgiveness, peace, hope, and love into her husband's life.

Throughout our marriage, Kim and I have faced many challenges. In those moments, we chose to touch and agree in prayer, and time after time, God showed up and performed miracles in our lives.

A man who really loves his wife:

- *Humbly asks for her support* in his spiritual growth
- *Values her prayers* and acknowledges their impact on his life
- *Seeks her wisdom* and insight as he grows into his calling
- *Partners with her in prayer* to face life's challenges together

By embracing his wife's role in his spiritual journey, he allows God to refine and shape him through their partnership, leading him to become the man God designed him to be.

Seek Help When Challenges Arise

When a man really loves a woman, he will seek out support when there's a conflict in the marriage. Every covenant relationship rooted in agape love will inevitably face trials, tests, suffering, difficulties, and challenges. No relationship is immune to conflict. However, when disagreements flare out of control, a man who really loves a woman takes responsibility for finding the help they need to heal and grow stronger together.

This means being proactive in seeking wise counsel—whether from trusted friends, pastors, professional counselors, marriage conferences, retreats, or mentoring relationships. I personally have a counselor on speed dial and another saved in my email for quick access during emergencies. As a marriage consultant with a doctoral degree in pastoral care and counseling, I fully understand the importance of seeking help when it's needed.

Despite my professional background, my wife and I still prioritize attending counseling sessions monthly to ensure we are constantly improving and nurturing our marriage. A man who truly loves his wife must do everything within his power to reduce conflict, not create or prolong it.

I often say that marriages should never settle for being status quo—

they should be thriving day after day, week after week. One critical way to cultivate a thriving marriage is by minimizing conflict and resolving issues swiftly and lovingly, allowing the relationship to return to the healthy, God-honoring bond it was designed to be.

A man who really loves a woman will:

- *Acknowledge when help is needed* and actively seek it
- *Prioritize peace and healing* over pride and stubbornness
- *Engage in regular check-ins* through counseling or mentorship
- *Commit to growth* in the relationship rather than settling for comfort

Seeking help is not a sign of weakness—it's a sign of wisdom, strength, and love. A man who pursues peace and growth ensures that his marriage will continue to thrive and reflect the love of Christ.

* * *

As we explore how to cultivate a spiritually strong marriage, we see the impact of building a relationship firmly rooted in God's love and truth. However, even in Christ-centered marriages, challenges and mistakes will arise, reminding us of our humanity. That's why forgiveness and grace are essential elements of any thriving relationship.

In the next chapter, we'll dive into the heart of practicing forgiveness and extending grace daily—two transformative acts that reflect God's love and pave the way for healing, restoration, and a deeper connection with your spouse.

HOW TO PRACTICE FORGIVENESS AND GRACE DAILY

A s the leader of the home, it's important for a man who really loves a woman to create a safe and nurturing environment where she can grow without feeling the pressure to be perfect. He forgives her mistakes, offering grace without allowing past errors to cause lingering damage in the relationship. This kind of forgiveness is a reflection of the command in God's Word:

 And be kind to one another, tenderhearted, forgiving one another, even as God in Christ forgave you.

— EPHESIANS 4:32

Forgiving trust is essential in a loving relationship. When forgiveness is absent, offense takes root in the heart, slowly eroding trust and intimacy. John Bevere wisely calls offense "the bait of Satan." It's a trap designed to divide and destroy.

This is how it works:

1. *Hurtful Words Occur:* Your spouse says something that causes pain.
2. *The Enemy Whispers Lies:* The enemy tempts you to stay offended— "You have the right to be angry. Stay hurt. Don't forgive."
3. *A Choice Must Be Made:* At this point, the hurt is just a feeling, and the temptation is a suggestion. Your next step is critical.

Feelings vs. Responses:

- *Feelings* are neither right nor wrong; they are emotional signals.
- *Responses* determine whether healing or harm will follow.

You can choose to respond with:

- Love or hate
- Forgiveness or bitterness
- Peace or Conflict

Your response determines whether you take the bait of offense or resist it. Remember, the enemy's goal is to steal your joy, destroy intimacy, and kill your relationship. But the enemy can only work through lies and temptation—you have the power to reject both.

The Word of God offers the key to resisting this trap:

> Therefore submit to God. Resist the devil and he will flee from you. Draw near to God and He will draw near to you. Cleanse your hands, you sinners; and purify your hearts, you double-minded.

> — James 4:7-8

A man who loves his wife will:

- *Earn Her Trust:* By consistently keeping his promises and being a man of integrity.
- *Forgive Her Mistakes:* Offering grace freely, without holding past failures against her.
- *Build a Safe Space:* Where she feels secure in his love, knowing she doesn't need to be perfect.
- *Model Christ's Love:* Showing kindness, compassion, and forgiveness as Christ forgave us.

Forgiveness is a choice, and trust is built over time. A man who really loves a woman understands that both are essential for a strong, lasting relationship.

PRACTICE THE FIVE LANGUAGES OF APOLOGY

A man who really loves a woman understands the power of a sincere apology. Apology is essential to forgiveness and is a critical step toward healing and restoring a relationship. Without it, unresolved hurt can create distance and resentment.

I highly recommend *The Five Languages of Apology* by Gary Chapman and Jennifer Thomas. While we can't explore every detail here, this framework offers a powerful guide to meaningful apologies that foster healing and reconciliation. These are the words every loving man should use to repair, restore, and strengthen his relationship:

1. Expressing Regret: "I am sorry."

- Acknowledging the pain you caused and showing genuine remorse for your actions.
- Example: *"I'm truly sorry for what I said. I know it hurt you."*

2. Accepting Responsibility: "I was wrong."

- Owning your mistake without excuses or shifting blame.
- Example: "I was wrong to speak to you that way. It wasn't right."

3. Making Restitution: "What can I do to make it right?"

- Taking steps to repair the damage and show your commitment to change.
- Example: "I realize I hurt you. How can I make this right?"

4. Genuinely Repenting: "I'll try not to do that again."

- Demonstrating a sincere desire to change your behavior.
- Example: "I am working on changing this, and I'll do everything I can to not let it happen again."

5. Requesting Forgiveness: "Will you please forgive me?"

- Humbly asking for forgiveness, recognizing that it's her choice to offer it.
- Example: "I know I hurt you. Will you please forgive me?"

A man who loves a woman prioritizes reconciliation over pride. He doesn't justify his mistakes or minimize her feelings. Instead, he humbly and intentionally seeks to repair the relationship with sincerity and care.

The Word of God reminds us:

 He who covers his sins will not prosper, but whoever confesses and forsakes them will have mercy.

— Proverbs 28:13

By practicing these five languages of apology, a man shows his commitment to nurturing trust, healing wounds, and building a foundation of love and grace. Apologizing isn't a sign of weakness—it's a mark of strength and genuine love.

TAKE THE "7 STEPS OF REPENTANCE"

When a man really loves a woman, he takes full responsibility for his actions and is committed to rebuilding trust without casting blame or making excuses. Genuine repentance is more than saying "I'm sorry"— it's a heartfelt process of change that fosters healing and restores trust.

> For godly sorrow produces repentance leading to salvation, not to be regretted; but the sorrow of the world produces death.
>
> For observe this very thing, that you sorrowed in a godly manner: What diligence it produced in you, what clearing of yourselves, what indignation, what fear, what vehement desire, what zeal, what vindication! In all things you proved yourselves to be clear in this matter.
>
> Therefore, although I wrote to you, I did not do it for the sake of him who had done the wrong, nor for the sake of him who suffered wrong, but that our care for you in the sight of God might appear to you.
>
> — 2 CORINTHIANS 7:10-12

Here are the 7 Steps of Repentance, each accompanied by affirmations that reflect a sincere desire for transformation:

1. Earnestness

- "I am eager to be transparent and clear myself with God."
- "I am running to repentance, seeking God in prayer and confession."
- "I weep sincere tears of sorrow, not because I was caught but because I truly desire to change."
- "I am committed to immediate and lasting change."

2. Eagerness to Clear Myself

- "I willingly release and refuse to revisit the baggage of the past."
- "I am ready to live a clean life, free from sin and compromise."
- "I will not give the enemy a foothold in my life or relationship."
- "I choose boldness in Christ over defensiveness or shame."

3. Indignation

- "I am disgusted by my wrongdoing and take full responsibility."
- "I am determined to crucify my flesh and resist temptation."
- "I have holy revulsion toward sin and the damage it causes."
- "I want to purge every toxic behavior and emotion from my life, especially any anger toward my beloved."

4. Alarm

- "I am humbled and filled with reverent fear of God."
- "I am alarmed by how sin has deceived me and damaged our relationship."
- "I recognize how pride and spiritual blindness have hindered me."
- "I am deeply distressed by my lack of vigilance and how it has affected my love for God and my beloved."

5. Longing

- "I long to love God and my beloved with all my heart, soul, mind, and strength."
- "I am passionately pursuing holiness and purity."
- "I yearn to have my integrity and innocence restored."

- "I constantly desire God's presence to surround and strengthen our relationship."

6. Concern (Zeal)

- "I pray for God's zeal to ignite passion and commitment in our covenant relationship."
- "I am wholeheartedly dedicated to pleasing God in every aspect of our relationship."
- "I am passionately in love with God and my beloved."
- "I am eager and determined to restore our relationship."
- "I recognize that I cannot live in peace without restoring our bond."

7. Readiness to See Justice Done

- "I trust the Lord to bring healing and justice into our relationship."
- "I am committed to making restitution and righting my wrongs."
- "I humbly ask for your forgiveness for the pain I have caused."
- "I will take actionable steps to rebuild trust and strengthen our relationship."

True repentance isn't passive—it's an active, heartfelt response to wrongdoing. Each of these seven steps reflects a man's sincere commitment to restoring what was broken and fostering an atmosphere of trust, love, and healing.

God's Word reminds us:

 Confess your trespasses to one another, and pray for one another, that you may be healed. The effective, fervent prayer of a righteous man avails much.

— JAMES 5:16

When a man really loves a woman, he does everything in his power to rebuild trust and renew love. He chooses accountability over excuses, humility over pride, and healing over division. This is the path to lasting love, grace, and restoration.

Admit Your Wrongs & Make Positive Changes

When a man really loves a woman, he is willing to admit his wrongs, quit them, and change any negative thoughts, feelings, and behaviors that cause hurt in the marriage. Admit, quit, and change are three essential actions a man must take to continually grow and become the best version of himself for the woman he loves. A man who truly loves his wife recognizes when his actions have caused pain and takes full responsibility. He doesn't make excuses—he acknowledges his mistakes, commits to stop harmful behaviors, and actively works to change.

When hurt occurs in a relationship, forgiveness becomes a vital step toward healing and rebuilding trust. True love requires humility and a willingness to change for the better.

The Bible emphasizes this:

> If we confess our sins, He is faithful and just to forgive us our sins and to cleanse us from all unrighteousness.
>
> — 1 John 1:9

A man who really loves a woman embraces this truth, knowing that admitting his faults, seeking forgiveness, and making lasting changes strengthens their bond and fosters a marriage built on trust, grace, and unconditional love.

Be A Peacemaker

When a man really loves a woman, he allows the Spirit of God to trans-

form him into a peacemaker. Peacemaking begins with repentance and forgiveness.

As previously stated, Ruth Bell Graham wisely said, "A happy marriage is the union of two good forgivers." When both partners commit to forgiving one another, they are transformed into peacemakers—serving each other with the same gladness they serve the Lord.

A man who really loves a woman intentionally fosters a peaceful atmosphere in their home. Every single day, he makes it a priority to create an environment where love can deepen and flourish. He leads by example, ensuring their home is a place of rest, refuge, and peace.

The Word of God instructs:

> Husbands, love your wives and do not be bitter toward them.
>
> — COLOSSIANS 3:19

Loving your wife unconditionally means cultivating peace, not toxicity. A man who really loves his wife seeks to protect the harmony of their relationship. He allows the Holy Spirit to guide him in being patient, gentle, and kind, ensuring that their marriage is built on a foundation of love, grace, and peace.

* * *

As we conclude our exploration of practicing forgiveness and grace, we recognize that these virtues are not just about healing relationships—they are also about becoming more like Christ. Extending forgiveness and grace requires humility, strength, and a willingness to grow into the person God has called you to be.

In the next and final chapter, we'll reflect on how to embrace God's design for your life as a man, husband, and leader. Together, we'll uncover the steps to align your heart with His purpose, so you can truly love, lead, and serve in a way that honors God and strengthens your marriage.

.

How to Become the Man God Designed You to Be

Throughout this book, we've explored how a man who truly loves a woman demonstrates that love through intentional actions, selfless commitment, and unwavering devotion. As we conclude, I want to leave you with a heartfelt reminder and practical steps that love is a daily, intentional choice.

Gary Chapman's *5 Love Languages* remain foundational in understanding how to love deeply and meaningfully. These five areas include:

- Words of Affirmation
- Quality Time
- Gift Giving
- Acts of Service
- Physical Touch

Here are some practical steps to show her that you love her:

1. Pay Attention to What She Loves

When a man really loves a woman, he pays close attention to the small details that bring her joy.

- *Gift Giving:* Learn the types of gifts that make her feel special. For example, I know my wife loves perfume. I've memorized her favorite scents and keep a list on my phone to surprise her with a "just because" gift.

- *Know Her Style:* Pay attention to the flowers she loves, the colors she prefers, and the style of décor she enjoys. Whether it's modern, rustic, or minimalist, knowing these details shows how much you care.

- *Special Dates:* Remember important dates—her birthday, anniversaries, and other meaningful occasions. Celebrate her achievements and milestones with thoughtfulness.

2. Be Intentional with Quality Time

- Take her to her favorite restaurants and plan experiences you know she'll enjoy.

- Schedule regular date nights and spontaneous getaways.

- Engage in her favorite hobbies or join her on morning walks, just to be by her side.

3. Speak Words That Affirm Her

- Learn and use the affirming words she loves to hear.

- Write her love letters, leave thoughtful notes, or send heartfelt texts.

- Compliment her sincerely and often.

4. Prioritize Physical Touch and Intimacy

- Show affection through holding hands, hugs, kisses, and thoughtful touches.

- Be proactive in maintaining physical intimacy. Address any challenges with care, even seeking medical support if necessary.

- Create intentional spaces for connection, like adding a massage table to the bedroom or planning romantic evenings.

5. Perform Acts of Service

- Help with household tasks without being asked.

- Support her emotionally and spiritually through thoughtful gestures.

- Anticipate her needs and go out of your way to lighten her load.

When a man really loves a woman, he anchors his love for her in the unwavering foundation of God's love. This means leading with humility, serving with grace, and cherishing her with a love that mirrors Christ's love for the Church. Rooting his love in God ensures that his devotion remains steadfast through life's challenges and joys, offering her a safe, nurturing, and spiritually uplifting relationship.

 For the commandments, 'You shall not commit adultery,' 'You shall not murder,' 'You shall not steal,' 'You shall not bear false witness,' 'You shall not covet,' and if there is any other commandment, are all summed up in this saying, namely, 'You shall love your neighbor as yourself.'

Love does no harm to a neighbor; therefore, love is the fulfillment of the law.

— Romans 13:9-10

God's agape love is our greatest example. His love is unconditional, constant, and overflowing. When a man loves a woman through God's lens, his love becomes a steady, life-giving force that never runs dry. A woman who is truly loved experiences a deep reservoir of love within her that brings peace, security, and joy.

 We love Him because He first loved us.

— 1 John 4:19

* * *

As this chapter—and this book—concludes, remember that true love is not passive; it is an active, daily choice to reflect God's unconditional love in your marriage. By aligning your heart with His purpose, you create a bond that is not only unshakable but also deeply fulfilling, both for you and the woman you love. Let your love be a reflection of God's design for marriage, leaving a legacy of faith, hope, and enduring commitment for generations to come.

Now, go love her well!

CLOSING PRAYER

Dear God,

Thank You for being our amazing Creator and Father. We humbly ask for forgiveness for the times we have fallen short in our relationships and for neglecting the things You have called us to do.

Lord, bless the readers of this book. Let them not only hear these truths but live them out daily. Strengthen marriages and relationships. Bring break-throughs, healing, and restoration. Help us to love selflessly and pursue our partners with the same intentionality and passion that You have shown us.

May our love reflect Your grace, mercy, and unconditional love. Let our actions honor You and bring peace to our homes.

In the Name of Jesus Christ, we pray.

Amen.

ACKNOWLEDGMENTS

I am thankful to God for this opportunity to share this manuscript, believing it will make a difference in individual lives and in the relationships between spouses—both within my immediate context and beyond!

To my anointed and amazing wife, *Kimberely Reeder Allen,* my biggest cheerleader, incredible prayer warrior, and unwavering supporter—thank you for your love, patience, and consistent strength in what God instructs me to do. You are the inspiration for this book! I often say, and will always say, that I thank God for allowing me the blessed privilege and opportunity to love you in such an amazing way, one day at a time, for a lifetime!

To my sons, *Jonathan W. Allen, Jr.* (the networker and connector) and *James R. Reeder* (the deep thinker); my grandson, *Jaquan J. McShay* (the hard worker); and my granddaughter, *Iyona Reeder* (the high-achiever) — you constantly push me outside of my comfort zone to be who God has called me to be. Thank you for staying connected and challenging me to grow. I pray that my life continues to serve as a reflection of God's love and a role model for your own spiritual and personal growth.

To my father, *Joseph Allen, Jr.,* who passed on November 21, 1993—I acknowledge the deep sense of manhood you instilled in me in just 29 years of my life. Your legacy continues to live on in the way I love my wife tremendously, and I pray I honor the values you taught me every day.

To my friend of 40-plus years, *Dr. Leroy Mack, III*—thank you for your unwavering support of this manuscript. Your wisdom, counsel, and input are always invaluable, and I deeply appreciate your presence in my life.

I thank God for my wonderful *Connect Church family*, where I have the blessed privilege of serving as Lead Pastor in Waldorf, Maryland. I simply say what all pastors cannot always say: *I love being your Pastor!*

I am deeply grateful for the people who have inspired and encouraged me in my journey of understanding and sharing about love and relationships. Two men, in particular, left an indelible mark on my heart and my perspective on what it truly means to love well: James (Jimmy) O'Grady and Kevin (Chef Kev) Branch, Sr.

Jimmy, who passed on February 25, 2017, was an exceptional husband, father, and man of integrity. I had the privilege of working closely with him and his wife, Denise O'Grady, and their love for one another was evident in everything they did. I vividly remember how they would talk on the phone at least ten times a day, ending every call with "I love you." Jimmy's unwavering commitment to expressing his love openly and consistently continues to inspire me and countless others.

Chef Kev was another extraordinary example of love in action. Kevin passed on August 15, 2024. During our friendship, I witnessed his unconditional and passionate love for his wife, Eva Branch, of forty-four years. He honored her with devotion, care, and dignity, modeling what it looks like to truly cherish one's partner.

I thank God for placing these men in my life. Their lives and marriages were a living testament to the power of love, and they have challenged and encouraged me to strive for that same standard of devotion in my own relationship. Their legacy serves as a reminder that true love is not just felt—it is demonstrated, nurtured, and celebrated daily.

To my editor and publisher, *Nicole Queen* of Vision Publishing House, who did an amazing job on this project— thank you for your expertise and dedication. I wholeheartedly recommend you to anyone who desires to write and publish their book!

ABOUT THE AUTHOR

Dr. Jonathan W. Allen, Sr., a native of Washington, D.C., is a devoted husband, proud father and grandfather, accomplished entrepreneur, and passionate author. A product of both public and private education in the District, he utilized his athletic talents to attend Elon College on scholarship. Dr. Allen holds a Bachelor's Degree from Nyack College, a Master of Divinity from Virginia Union University, and a Doctor of Ministry in Pastoral Care & Counseling, with a specialization in relationship consulting, pre-marital counseling, and marriage enrichment, from United Theological Seminary in Dayton, Ohio.

With a heart for helping couples build strong, faith-centered relationships, Dr. Allen draws on decades of experience to inspire and equip others with the tools to thrive in love and life.

* * *

To get in contact with Dr. Allen:

Email: DrJWAllenSr@gmail.com
Phone: 301-778-0711

www.ingramcontent.com/pod-product-compliance
Lightning Source LLC
Chambersburg PA
CBHW051523120626
46551CB00012B/1056